TRANSCENDING UTOPIA

Reopening the
Pathway to Divinity

KEVIN HUNTER

WARRIOR
OF LIGHT
PRESS

Warrior of Light Press
www.kevin-hunter.com

Body, Mind & Spirit/Spiritualism
Inspiration & Personal Growth
New Thought

Dedication

This is for you on your spiritual journey in transcending utopia. May you be blessed with the gifts of love, knowing, sensing, hearing, and seeing for the purpose of the greater good of your higher self and humanity.

CHAPTERS

KEVIN HUNTER

AUTHOR'S NOTE

Transcending Utopia is infused with practical messages and guidance that my Spirit team has taught and shared with me revolving around many different topics. The main goal is to fine-tune your body, mind and soul. You are a Divine communicator capable of receiving messages and guidance from Heaven, as all souls are regardless if they believe in that or not.

The messages, guidance, information, and topics included in this book are areas that my Spirit team has guided me to discuss. My team makes up God and the Holy Spirit, as well as a team of guides, angels, and sometimes Archangels and Saints. I am merely the liaison or messenger in delivering and interpreting the intentions of what they wish to communicate.

I was born with dominating Clairaudience and Claircognizance, with varying degrees of Clairsentience and Clairvoyance. My Spirit team comprises some hard truth telling Wise Ones from the other side, including Saint Nathaniel, who can be brutal in his truthful forcefulness. He cuts right to the heart of humanity without apology. I have learned quite a bit from him while adopting his ideology, which is Heaven's philosophy as a whole.

If I use the word "He" when pertaining to God, this does not mean that I am advocating that he is a male. Simply replace the word; "He" with one you are comfortable using to identify God for you to be. If the word, "God" makes you uncomfortable, then substitute it with one you're more familiar with. This goes for any gender I use as examples. When I say, "spirit team", I am referring to a team of 'Guides and Angels'.

One of the purposes of my work is to empower, enlighten, as well as entertain. It's to help you improve yourself, your soul, your life and humanity as a result. It does not matter if you are a beginner or well versed in the subject matter. There may be something that reminds you of something you already know or something that you were unaware of. We all have much to share with one another, as we are all one in the end.

~ Kevin Hunter

TRANSCENDING UTOPIA

CHAPTER ONE

Opening the Pathway to Divinity

Connecting with my Divine Spirit team through Channeling sometimes requires taking a deep breath in if I'm not relaxed, followed by shutting my eyes on the exhale. The second my eyes close, the connection is dramatically established as if pushing an electrical plug into a wall socket that creates a spark. The initial connection entails being immediately catapulted through the air similar to a cannonball firing. It can move in numerous ways where I'm soaring at lightning speed through the vortex portal only to slam into an ocean plummeting downwards deeper and faster into its dark watery depths that accelerates in a fashion comparable to a rocket gaining steam, then the messages float in.

One of the other ways is the missile firing is followed by a bomb explosion going off leaving me surrounded by brilliant shining bright white light. This is only to realize I've been moving at rapid speed within it. The light breaks apart and dissolves into billions of stars. This interstellar display evaporates and the laws of human physics are defied as I ascend higher by means of what some call astral travel and projection. This intergalactic travelling through light years of galaxy and space is where the messages sift into my consciousness.

I have no idea where I'll be taken until I shut my eyes only to discover my vessel is travelling upwards or downwards. The chilling transporting happens if I'm sent into the depths of the ocean, as there is a few second shock and fear of potential drowning. This is followed by a heaviness that luckily subsides into contentment the further I plunge into its intense profoundness. Crossing into the portal I'm surrounded by council in a comfortable gigantic wave of strengthening love like being hugged to death. Everything grows exceedingly calm while in its brilliant transcending radiance.

Your Vibration and Consciousness

Your consciousness needs to be awakened enough to allow you to see profound truths. No one can awaken your consciousness except you. It is the individual soul's job to do the work, research, study, and experience in order to strengthen your soul essence. This means not following the masses, but breaking away from the collective to find your personal soul path.

You are made up of energy the same way everything is made up of energy. How you direct that energy will dictate the essence of what will come back to you. If your feelings and thoughts are negative, then what is soon brought into your life is what matches that vibration. If your thoughts and feelings are positive, then this is the energy that is eventually brought into your life. There is no set time frame on how quick or slow something of equal or greater value to the energy matched with your feelings and thoughts is brought into your life.

A raised vibration coupled with life experience helps in awakening your consciousness. When your consciousness is awakened, you view Earthly life with a broader perception. Suddenly Earthly life in general appears trivial and superficial. You may start to feel permanently disconnected from it, isolated, and set apart from the norm. While this might cause you to stumble into a depression, understand that these are clues that your consciousness is expanding.

A raised consciousness gives you a wider perception that allows room for stronger cognitive input. This is the area where information from above falls into and is planted.

Your vibration is made up of undetectable cells to the human eye. These cells fluctuate and change colors depending on your mood, your thought processes, who you surround yourself with, as well as what you ingest into your body. Your vibration is an invisible energy field that exists within the DNA of your soul, aura, and physical body. You are in control of this vibration energy field. It is up to you to oversee this vibration energy and dictate how well you would like it to function.

It's the same way you control other parts of your life such as the car you drive, to the house or apartment you live in, and so on. When you maintain your car, then you ensure it runs smoothly with routine check-ups, oil changes, checking the tire pressure, etc. This is similar to you taking care of your physical health as best as possible from getting regular check-ups, to watching the diet you consume, exercising regularly, to your overall daily state of mind. Taking care of your physical body affects your spiritual body. It's watching your thoughts and feelings to ensure they are on the positive side. All of this affects how bright or dim the energy field of your vibration radiates.

A High and Low Vibrational State

Your vibration can drop when you fall into a challenging negative state, which will happen on occasion. You get caught up in the routine and day-to-day practicalities of life and experiences that it leaves no room to check up on you, and how you're doing, and what your soul needs. The soul craves nourishment and the ego will at times interfere prompting you to reach for toxic substances to temporarily feed it, but which ultimately drain you leaving you wanting more.

When your vibration is low, you feel and experience negative feelings such as anger, depression, stress, irritability, and so on. When your vibration is high, you feel euphoric feelings of joy, love, peace, and contentment.

While in a higher vibration state, you'll find that what you desire moves into your vicinity quicker than if your well-being state was on the negative side. Your psychic intuitive awareness then grows allowing the heavenly spirit answers, messages, and guidance to come into your consciousness and through your psychic clair channels on a clearer level. The messages and guidance you receive is what helps you make sounder choices in your life.

A vibration in spiritual concepts is your overall emotional well-being and energetic state. Feelings such as depression, anger, and guilt lower your vibration, but if you're feeling joyful, in love, and centered, then your vibration begins to rise. The lowest vibrational state includes feelings of anger, stress, or depression. Watch out if you're experiencing a combination of all three at once.

The highest vibrational states are feelings of peace, joy, and love. It isn't a surprise that those traits are synonymous with the Christmas holiday season as a reminder to not forget your natural state of being. Experiencing all three of those states at the same time makes you a high vibrational powerhouse! Love is the highest vibrational state possible, so always revert to raising your emotional state to that of love.

You are born in a perfect state of high vibrational energy. Somewhere along the way rough tumultuous Earthly life circumstances shake your faith while knocking your vibration down in the process. When you're conscious of when this happens, then you can quickly re-align your vibration. I understand how hard that can be for those that live tougher stress filled lives. No one is exempt from Earthly life challenges, including the rich and famous. Even they are faced with their own challenges that might be similar or dissimilar to yours on a personal level outside of having financial riches. It's tough for some people to feel sympathy for someone who is financially well off, but no one is above or below anyone else in spiritual truth. No one gets a free pass from Earthly life challenges. Some of those challenges are ego self-induced, while others are spiritual lessons to help you grow and evolve.

Be mindful of your well-being state whenever possible, because a low vibration alters the energetic field around you. This blocks both divine guidance and positive circumstances from entering your vicinity. It tampers with your life on a spiritual and physical level. Being in a perpetual negative mood state can have health related consequences. When you have a high vibration, then positive experiences flow into your life. Your psychic antennae with the Other Side is also sharper where you're able to pick up on the messages and guidance coming in swiftly than if you were in a low vibration state.

Seeking the Path Towards Enlightenment

The lifelong battle with demons in my personal life is always matched with those from beyond the veil consistently pointing me towards the Light. When touched by the power, it is unconditional love experienced that no words can describe. The soul is overwhelmed in that radiance when enveloped in its arms. The answer to the question of the meaning of life is always the same. The answer is LOVE.

The more enlightened you become, and the more you raise your consciousness, then the better off you'll be. This doesn't mean that you'll be stress free, but you'll certainly experience less stress while being able to efficiently navigate through the treacherous waters of the practical world easier than if you did not have that raised consciousness.

Imagine if every human soul found the gift of love within them. No one would need to be here since that would be Utopia. When you find the space of love and learn to keep it there and revert to it when possible, then the closer you are to creating Heaven on Earth. It's a beautiful thing when one soul awakens another in a positive way just by being in their presence.

The rays of God's Light activate the soul propelling you into a Utopian paradise and beyond. The ultimate Nirvana is surpassing that perfection through methods a limited consciousness could ever dream possible. This is the exceptional glory your soul was born into before the dense turbulence of Earthy life enveloped and suffocated you. Deep down every soul longs to re-attain and achieve that blissful excellence that gives the impression of unabashed joy and serenity. It is a condition where unwavering love and harmony surround you in a protected cushion. Transcending beyond the dull insensible frustrated Earthy life and into the natural condition the soul once habited is a goal that delights. It reminds the soul of where it came from. You runaway and travel around the globe searching for a sign of this utopia, only to be consistently left with disappointment. This is because utopia begins and ends inside the spark that burns within your soul like a pilot light.

Examine the negative emotions that initially impede your soul's movement. Start within and visualize this pilot light being ignited to the degree conceivable of generating a wildfire that expands in an explosion purging and clearing away all of the darkness the ego consistently loses itself in.

CHAPTER TWO

The Core Soul Groups, Soul Contracts, and Life Purposes

Endless data of information exists in every soul's contract. This contract is more than a sheet of paper or the kind of contract you expect to receive for a job position. The duties listed in a human job contract are not far off from the nature of the soul contract, which also lists duties and purposes you're agreeing to work towards accomplishing for the benefit of your soul. One core difference between the soul contract and a regular job contract is that you cannot get fired for not performing your soul duties. Every soul contract is large enough to fill numerous large books that house each soul's lifetimes on Earth, galaxies, and dimensions. These books reside in a place we call the Hall of Records in Heaven. Not only does the contract list your purposes and core events scheduled to take place, but everything you do or do not do is also recorded in this book.

While the terminology 'spirit world' is often used to illustrate the separate planes, in truth it's much more grand than that. Some believe the spirit world to be filled with ghostly spirits roaming around. On the contrary, it is the ultimate Utopian paradise that is an unbelievable spectacle. It mirrors the nature settings and natural wonders on Earth, but is even more vibrant, lush, and magical than the human mind could comprehend. It would have to be because why would a place full of 100% uplifting joy, love, and peace be less than the physical Earthly plane? The Earthly plane is a school set up that houses spirits of every variety in a human body. All souls on Earth are students, with a smaller percentage being both student and teacher. This is because even a teacher is a student learning new things while living an Earthly life.

There are three core human soul groups:

• Baby Souls. Those are the souls causing the greatest harm on Earth. They use the maximum amount of darkness of ego. They're the ones that harm, hurt, or hate. They start wars, incite violence, and destruction on the planet or on other beings. Many are the criminals on Earth, but there are also souls who are not criminals, yet cause quite a bit of heartache or disaster on others.

• Mid-Level Souls. Those are the ones just trying to get by and survive. They are trying to make it through an Earthly life. Their purposes are geared towards working hard on one or many aspects of themselves. They may be on the planet to live an Earthly life and follow the human customs of that time such as getting a job, getting married, buying a house, having kids, etc. At some point one of these souls may start to question life in general and possibly receive an awakening that thrusts them to graduate and begin moving to a higher soul level.

• Evolved/Evolving Post Graduate Souls. These are the teachers or the ones bringing light and wisdom to others on some level. They enact positive change and tend to steer clear of the human ego trappings. Some of them may be fully evolved and here to live an Earthly life while bringing something positive to the planet. There will be other souls who are evolving out of the Mid-Level Soul branch and into this branch during their lifetime. Those are the ones also living several lifetimes in one. Many souls from the various realms that exist on the other side incarnate as an evolved or evolving soul to offer their services to the betterment of humanity.

Human Souls Operate on Different Levels

On Earth, there are hierarchy positions within some companies running from the CEO down to the executives, to the assistants, receptionists, and so on. What is interesting is that even though a CEO on Earth may be financially successful, they could be spiritually bankrupt. Their Earthly drive is for monetary success and nothing else. They could be considered a baby soul in the spiritual world, while their assistant may actually be a realm soul who Heaven knows to be an evolved/evolving, advanced, post-graduate soul, which in the end is what lasts. Only on Earth is the distribution of power imbalanced, or what human souls consider to being of power, since real power is spiritual competence.

A parent might be a baby soul ruling from the darkness of ego, while their child could be an evolving post-graduate soul who is much older in soul years than their own parent. This would be obvious where the parent seems to be more childlike in its tantrums, and the child coming off more wise, centered, or compassionate than its parent.

All human souls will die and when that happens they will be buried just like every other human soul that passes on. They will be buried without anything, but what they're dressed in. Even that will tarnish and grow old over time covering a physical body that disintegrates into the Earth's ground before becoming a set of bones. The soul that continues to live on will exit that body and immediately move towards the part of their soul's home where everyone is balanced. There is no such thing as power to get ahead in Heaven, because all souls live in peace and harmony. They're not fighting or killing one another off to get ahead.

Upon human death, the assistant that worked on Earth moves to a higher space of consciousness than the CEO on Earth did due to him not growing his soul. This is because in the spirit realms you move to areas where your soul group is. The soul group consists of your soul siblings who have similar gifts as you do and who are on the same soul growth level. You head back home to Heaven upon your Earthly death with newfound insight you gained while on Earth.

Living an Earthly life you are forced to engage with souls who are on various levels of soul growth that may be similar or dissimilar to you. What is immediately understood for you is the chaos that ensues on the physical world. Many souls on Earth struggle to get ahead and one up each other to prove they have the answers, when in reality few have only slices of truth.

Human beings ruling their life from the darkness of ego cause the majority of misery experienced. If every single soul on the planet were in tune and connected with the Divine full time, while using their God given born traits of love, then Earth would be as blissful as Heaven. This will unlikely happen since Earth is filled with Baby Souls. Those newborn souls that sparked out of God were quickly born into a human body for the sake of learning and growth on Earth.

Children throw tantrums when they don't get what they want and baby souls are no different. A baby soul can be in the body of a 70 year old human being. Just because the human being is appearing of older age it does not mean they're wise. It is still a baby soul who has experienced one lifetime at this Earth school. Depending how rapidly they evolved will determine where they will go upon their exit of the human vessel.

Some Earthly souls will display a higher range of their gifts than other souls, but it doesn't mean that other souls are incapable of that. All souls are the same inside as they came from the same Light. If they display less of the gift than another, then this is connected to having a block in the physical world, or it is compensated through having an ability displayed through another gift that someone else might have less of. All are born into an Earthly life with specific psychic gifts that are extra enhanced than another in order for them to use that for the purpose of the higher good. This benefit is also for them to pay attention to so that they can be guided along their Earthly path with minimal challenges as possible.

All souls will endure challenges as that is the nature of the beast that is the Earthly life. Those more in tune to the planes beyond will work harder to access their deep gifts in order to be able to move about through any Earthly challenges swifter than someone else who ignores those gifts.

Soul Contracts

Much of the challenges the soul endures are listed in the soul's contract book located in the Hall of Records on the other side. This Hall of Records is no ordinary library. It contains all the answers to anything and everything that a soul could possibly want to know. Placing your hand on it allows the information to be filtered rapidly into your soul's consciousness like a computer uploading data.

One of the many agreements contained in the soul contract has a set up that lays out numerous paths that branch out into other numerous roads. It looks like the LIFE board game, but is a hundred times more complex.

If you miss one fork in the road and head down a different path it might reveal that you would take the longer route around before you reach your destination. What is interesting is that the majority of the roads lead to the same destination, with a percentage of souls heading in a completely different direction due to the free will choice action of the individual.

An event intended to take place may be soul contracted, but no spirit being can interfere with your free will choice. This is still your life to live it for you. Your Spirit team will do their best to gently guide you towards the direction you originally agreed upon, but your ego can override that and choose to do what it wants you to do. As a result, you end up being taken for a ride in another direction.

Some paths take the longer away around, while others might have more challenges listed on them. There are also three exit points that indicate the main sections of your life where your soul may choose to exit this life and head back home. There are also agreements indicating the various soul mates you'll encounter along your life path. It also lists the purposes and intentions that you and each soul mate will have with one another. These include the numerous lessons you've both agreed to endure for the benefit of soul growth.

Because you have free will choice, this can negate and alter what is intended to take place. This contract may reveal a particular love soul mate showing up at a particular time. Due to free will choice on your part and/or this other person's part, it can alter and change both your paths pushing the connection further out, or from happening at all.

One example is it can be something such as remaining with a current partner that was supposed to end awhile back, but didn't for various reasons. The next partner soul mate rarely shows up before the previous one is absolutely without a doubt complete. In some cases, the next soul mate partnership does show up, but you both fail to acknowledge one another or pay attention due to having one foot cemented in the previous connection refusing to give up and walk away. You know that previous connection was supposed to end a long time ago because it's usually bathed in toxic unstable issues. Your free will choice can convince you to stay longer than you should have for fear of what might happen or not happen.

Other times, the ego will put you in a denial phase where you believe without a doubt this person is the one you're supposed to be with, but the other person is failing to see that. As a result, you cling to that person not realizing you had been deceived by the ego to drag it on longer than it was intended to. When it is the right person for you, there will be no resistance coming on either side. It will happen as natural as it would in a romantic comedy.

Sometimes the future soul mate love partner will show up while you're still in the connection that was supposed to end. You feel a strong gravitational pull towards that new person even though you might not romantically act on anything with them. Both teams of guides from your side and this other person's side are aware that the old connection is going to end, so they jump the gun and orchestrate the bumping into part of this new person knowing nothing might take off for awhile.

For some people, connections take time before having full lift off that it's safe enough to bring them in and let it take its time evolving into more down the line. Meanwhile, the former love connection has fulfilled its contract agreement and begins to disband. It isn't long before the new love interest begins to have lift off.

This is one example of the many possible scenarios that can take place. There are times where no lift off happens due to free will choice. The connection will be pushed further and further out. Sometimes it never happens and one of the soul's passes on. Should the soul decide to have another Earthly life along with that soul mate at or around the same time, they will both be listed again on the new soul contract in hopes of recognizing one another.

When two souls are ready and evolved enough, then the lifelong love partnership will happen when either least expects it. You will both be placed on the same path where it is orchestrated perfectly to the point you're both standing face to face. There is no way either of you cannot see it.

Detecting Your Souls Purpose

Not all life purposes are career related or a financial gaining one. Some life purposes are emotional traits learned, such as spending a lifetime learning how to easily forgive others over slights your ego feels they enacted on you. Forgiveness is one of the hardest action steps for a soul to reach. How do you forgive someone who took advantage of your good nature and seemingly destroyed an element of your life? It takes work and discipline to make your peace with someone that caused you turmoil. The sooner you do that, the quicker you evolve and move onto more important purposes.

Life purposes are easy to detect because it's one of the main goals that never seems to leave your mind throughout the years. For some, it is what gives you pleasure to dive into, but it can also be specific emotional traits that you struggle and wrestle with most of the days of your life, such as learning the act of forgiveness or reducing anger.

One life purpose example would be Albert Einstein and the work he contributed that assisted in prospering the planet. This doesn't mean all are called here to invent something. Many life purposes are geared towards acquiring soul enhancing traits such as gaining human life experience and the knowledge that it entails. This can be by learning responsibilities such as finding a job to pay your bills. There is more to Earthly life than finding a job and paying bills, but it's the learning responsibility act that is the knowledge gained that connects to your purpose. One should seek out a job that gives them pleasure and by default those around you. This isn't always an easy thing to do with the grave amount of competition fighting for the same role.

The sole cause of abundance blockage is fear. Some people will stay in what they perceive to be a dead end job for fear of biting the bullet and taking a risk to walk away and go after their life purpose work. Of course, you should never walk away from a job unless you know it's practically safe to do so. This means you are prepared for the worst-case scenario that could entail you not finding another job.

The best way to move your passion into a financially independent career is to work on it on the side while you have the security of your current job. Devote at least a small amount of work each day towards your side passion career, so that you don't feel as if you're wasting your life at a job you despise. The benefits to doing that are if it's your passion, then it doesn't feel like work.

It also gives you something positive to look forward to each day knowing you have this back up plan you're working on. If one day you suddenly lose your job due to being laid off or fired, then at least you have this passion career on the side you had been working on. It just may give you the push to dive into at full force once regular employment ceases to exist. It's never too late to think about and plan for your future.

It's not uncommon to feel like you don't want to be here anymore or that you feel your journey is complete. This is not always a fun world to live in. The misery created can be at the hands of those around you, but sometimes it can be you who is creating the misery without realizing it. If you're still here, then you are supposed to be, even if you have no clue as to why. It is your job and quest to discover why on your own. Ask yourself the important questions and examine your life to a hair splitting degree to come to the conclusion as to why you are here. Everyone on the planet has a purpose.

In a journal or email to yourself, jot down the significant life events that transpired for you to date. What did you learn or gain from that? Allow your soul to involve itself in the Earthly life school work so that you may graduate into other spheres of consciousness. No one can do it for you. It's the same methodology as going to Earth's grade school. You had to show up to class, pay attention, study, and take tests in order to pass. Earthly life school for your soul is similar in that you have to do the work, learn, grow, evolve, and graduate.

Earthly life is tough for millions of human souls who are working jobs that crush and kill their life force. Part of this is due to the current way that people have designed the modern day work world. There is a greater distinction between working a job in a corporate environment you despise as opposed to finding a job that brings out your passions, creativity, and enjoyment. There are many souls who feel at home in a corporate structured environment, but it should be with the goal of making a positive impact for others. The problem is most that fall into that structure become equally rigid failing to invite in healthy balance. This balance is something discussed in greater detail in my book, *Living for the Weekend*, which is devoted solely to balancing your spiritual personal life and your practical work and career.

CHAPTER THREE

Exhibiting Fearlessness

Everyone experiences some form of fear at some point if not on a regular basis. Most anything fear based isn't real. It still doesn't stop you from conjuring up fear about what will or will not come. It's a matter of recognizing fear, looking it in the eye, and then running it over not allowing it to consume you. Fear is the opposite of faith. Fear starts with a false thought from the ego, and then the soul follows willingly believing it. It takes time and practice devoted to training oneself to ignore the fear and walk in faith.

Fear is one of the leading causes of soul and personal failure. It brings on paralysis, chaos, and procrastination.

Moving past fear requires awareness of what you're attempting to defeat. Overcoming fear is no easy feat and can take a lifetime to conquer since the human soul has a built in ego. The ego is split into both the light and darkness of ego. The light ego being what gives you confidence to trust and believe in who you are and your abilities, while the darkness of ego twists that into greed, anger, or fear.

Every soul on the planet experiences fear throughout their Earthly life. It is the one common trait that everyone has listed in their soul contract before incarnating into an Earthly life. You're a feeling, breathing, thinking consciousness moving about in a physical vessel for a variety of reasons. Every single person on the planet has a reason for being here, even if you have no clue what it is at any given moment. It is up to you to discover your numerous purposes that are connected to one singular intention. There are the default motives that all are here such as learning to love, but there are other goals outside of that even though love is always at the top of the list in the end.

Where you are on the fear scale can range from the minimal to being consumed by a fear that drowns and paralyzes you. The more sensitive you are, then the more fear you are apt to brewing up inside. Use your sensitivities to your advantage and transmute any fear into self-confidence. Believe in yourself knowing that you are worthy if not more capable than any other to do what you are perpetually called to do.

One soul may be aware of internal fears and will ignore it by persevering anyway. Another soul will become crippled by fear and accomplish nothing in the process. The latter soul allows the grips of this invisible negative energy to plague their thoughts and entire being to the point of paralysis. The dreams they've always wanted to conquer never transpire due to this fear.

Fear breeds out of the ego, the part of you that gives you a sense of self worth. When left unchecked the ego will run uncontrollably initiating all sorts of chaos and drama. The ego thrives on drama and negativity. This is what gives the beast life. Fear is manifested from the darkness of ego the same way a female gives birth to its child. Fear begins to grow and expand during your childhood development and upbringing. If you grew up in a household where you were constantly being told you're no good and will never amount to anything, then as you grow older and set out to accomplish your life purpose, the fears that rise up from conquering your purpose will incessantly talk you out of it. The ego will talk you out of accomplishing anything positive by filling your mind with thoughts you heard from others growing up through adolescence. The dark ego says, "You can't do that, you're not qualified, you are wasting your time, and you will never be a success at anything."

The repetitive words forever sift through your mind preventing you from taking action and getting to work. This creates a block that prevents you from going after what you desire. It is a block that forms a wall intended to disconnect you from the Divine. The Divine is where the answers, messages, and guidance reside in to help you travel down a smoother path while here.

The Dangers of Fear Energy

One of the things to remember when channeling energy in a positive direction is to avoid getting caught up in the grips of fear. Fear energy is one of the most dangerous energies ever attributed to humankind. It has been amazingly excessive for centuries that it triggers all sorts of destruction on the planet and on each other. From the perspective of an angel, you can imagine what that looks like seeing comets darted around like a tennis ball getting everyone nowhere.

Fear and worry plague the planet to an unhealthy degree causing it to expand and shoot out into the universe only to dart right back down like a boomerang in an explosion. The fear and worry energy has been especially magnified due to how quickly information is transmitted through the media and online. This fear originates within all of the individual souls on Earth and multiplies creating a fire that burns and destroys everything in its wake. Fear and worry do nothing to help anyone.

Fear is one of the soul's worst enemies. It is the reason the planet is plagued with interpersonal and global battles. Fear is responsible for preventing you from achieving and conquering your purpose. Living in a space of fear is what blocks you from moving forward. Opportunities are lost due to fear because it ensures you remain paralyzed causing you to cower and hide from going after what you desire.

Fear stalls humanity from evolving as witnessed in the centuries of evolution on the planet. While progress continues to be made in diminutive trickles, improvement still moves at a glacial rate thanks to humanities fear. It should not take hundreds of years to advance in the tiniest steps despite taking what we can get. This is due to individual fear resisting against changing their perception and awakening their consciousness. Finding the space of love and respect is challenging for the mediocre mind. Training every breathing organism to snap out of it takes an army of lights to do their part. Extricate fear from your aura and become unstoppable.

I met a woman in her 60's who was a former bank manager who quit and moved into semi-retirement. She wanted to supplement her income by becoming a Real

Estate Agent on the side. The positive is she wouldn't have bank hours and could work when she chooses to on her own schedule. She walked into this new real estate career having zero experience not knowing the meaning of a counter offer. Six months after she started this new career, she was closing $1 million plus homes in beach coastal cities. After one year, I saw her face was on bus stop benches and billboards.

Some people say they're too old for something or not qualified and have no experience, but this woman is a testament that she could do it IF she wanted it bad enough. She wanted it bad enough and went after it with joy and passion, then conquered it in bigger ways anyone imagined.

Fear is a ridiculously powerful dark energy that keeps you spinning around in the same spot ensuring you get nowhere. It makes you hate others who are not like you and those that you don't understand. Those who are unusual and dissimilar from the norm are the souls ushering in positive change in their individual way. They avoid following the herd and seem to be pushed to the forefront alone. That is one clue that you are standing in front of a soul leader.

Fear is controlled by what spiritual circles call the Ego and religious circles call the Devil. Either way both are interchangeable to describe the same thing. The ego doesn't want to see you succeed and win. It wants to keep you feeling trapped and helpless. Work on releasing fears connected to anything in your life. Release it by handing it over to God, source, the universe, your higher self, the angels, your Spirit team, or whatever you're comfortable referring to it as.

You can say, "I don't want this, please take it. I'm not going to worry about this anymore. I'm going to let you do that while I focus on other things. And so it is."

Ignore the fear and run into the flames knowing you

may get burned, because at least you put yourself out there. You stood up for yourself by doing what you want to do. Your consciousness will be that much stronger, smarter, and powerful.

The attitude I've always had when diving into anything and everything I ever wanted fearlessly is to just dive on in. This means doing it anyway no matter what kind of fear energy attempts to get in the way. Nothing stops me when I'm operating from my highest self because I am suddenly worthy and qualified. That's not bad for someone who battles with social anxiety everyday. You may be afraid of jumping, yet you still do it anyway because it's worth the risk to at least try to conquer your dreams. Reach that place where you can look back on your life and say, "I am a long way from where I've been."

In my life's trek to wellness from the brink of ruin with drug and alcohol addiction, I have risen up again and again. You are stronger than whatever is trying to tear you down. Recovery is sublime good hard work worth any price. Summon the nerve to get back up after any misfortune and don't let your life pass you by where it results in you getting the feeling that you've missed the boat. It is never too late to start anything you truly want to do. You are more powerful than you realize.

Fighting the Fear

Many human souls have passion and heart, but will do nothing with that Divine given gift out of fear. Fear is the #1 cause of turmoil in human souls. Fear comes from the ego and prevents you from going after your life purpose, your dream job, or the love interest. It is fear to speak your truth lovingly, or fear that stops you from going out and accomplishing things.

Some wrestle with anxiety due to their heightened sensitivities to the stimuli around them. Those with higher traits of anxiety, tend to be more in tune, psychic, or intuitive than other souls. They absorb more than the average person absorbs, and for that matter need to adopt a strict disciplined routine that is aligned with their personal equilibrium. Use your emotions to your advantage, since they house communication receptors with the Divine.

Anxiety rises when fear becomes too great, but most fears are outlandish, meaning that what you fear tends to be exaggerated. Notice what makes you fearful about something, then examine what that is to a high degree and note if the cause is more in your head rather than based in truth.

Sometimes it's not necessarily fear of failure, but fear of success that you're undeserving of rewards. You might feel guilty about it, but everyone deserves success and rewards. No soul is more special than another in the eyes of Heaven. Opportunities exist for you to take hold of and run with in the right spirit.

The same fear is associated with the risk of pursuing a potential love interest. You might be afraid to approach your crush for fear of being rejected, but if it's someone you can't get your mind off of, then take the risk to at least say hello to this person. Gauge their interest level after saying hello and notice if they seem standoffish because they're not interested or unfriendly due to shyness. Some people have given up a potential love interest that is intended for them out of fear, or they'll avoid approaching a potential partner out of fear. Fear is one of the greatest causes of human sabotage holding people back.

Many ignore the windows of opportunity revealed to them by spirit, thus watching life race on by. Don't allow opportunities and blessings placed in front of you to go unnoticed. You don't want to reach a place at the end of your life where you have regrets wishing you would've gone after something, or taken a risk on what you desire.

I've always been a fan of the fearless and the courageous, even if they know they'll fall flat on their face. I love seeing anyone walk through fire no matter what because nothing holds them back. They stand in their soul's power. If they fall, they pay no mind and get back up and keep going as if it's no big deal. They're fearless and continue to stand strong in the face of any setbacks or calamity.

Mastering fearless confidence on Earth can be challenging with the endless toxic negative energy being darted at you from all angles. Sometimes you create that negativity with the power of your own mind. Your worries and fears are unfounded since in the end all is always well. In Heaven, all souls are fearless and confident. There is no lower energy that permeates their aura like it does on Earth.

Archangel Michael – The Extractor of Fear

The Archangel Michael is God's right hand security general that oversees all beings, including Warrior of Light's, all archangels, and angels. Many Warriors souls have Archangel Michael around them since he is one of the strongest most fearless beings in the Heavens. He might assist with extracting fear from a soul while helping them to rise to confidence when their lower self gets in the way. He is also their protector to ensure they are not harmed by anyone. Warrior of Light's invite in antagonism from the lower evolved who feel threatened by them. It is beneficial to have Michael in your house to extract the lower energies out of your vicinity.

Archangel Michael is the loudest entity I've ever come across. He is the only entity louder than God, while stretching to appear as tall as 30 to 40 feet and sometimes taller to make his presence known. He is often depicted in artwork as standing on or holding down a hideous monstrous devil like creature without effort. This can be the Devil itself or the darkness of ego in individual souls.

There are moments where I can be accused of being cocky. This is someone who might come off arrogantly overconfident and bold. Archangel Michael is with me every day of my life and ironically this is his principal energy. Only someone's ego would be ruffled over another who exudes superhuman confidence.

Archangel Michael struts around almost like a boastful rooster alpha male. Calling him overconfident is too little of a word to describe his self-assurance. When he's not extracting lower energies and people away with his light sword, he's showing off like a male peacock. Sometimes the light around him bursts into a brightly colored light show for no reason at all except to show off the way a male peacock does. This is similar to Archangel Michael's basic nature when he's not diving into battle fearlessly for God.

Call upon Archangel Michael for intervention when you are drowning in fear, anxiety, self-doubt, or lacking in confidence.

People believe what they want to believe and there is nothing you can do about it. Thinking in a limited way is the kiss of death. Communicating with any angel or archangel is communicating with God. They are His arms and hands, so even if you don't feel you are communicating to God, you are. The best parts of the human soul are of God. The darkness of ego is not. You can't run away from God. Michael isn't more superior than God, since he is of God and a part of God. Michael is so powerful and loud that he comes off more superior than God, even though they are one in the same. This soldier angel is present in a big way!

Archangel Michael has always been around over the centuries, but now more than ever. The darkness is particularly heightened due to how rapidly it spreads through technology, which is why Michael has called on souls to come into this lifetime to fight the darkness of ego that exists in others.

If you're experiencing a negative entity hanging around you, call on Archangel Michael and request that he bring the entity into the light. If you're feeling enormous fear, then bring in Archangel Michael to help lift you into bold confidence. Know that you are more powerful than you might give yourself credit for. Rise to the task of becoming the natural born fearless warrior soul you were made to be.

CHAPTER FOUR

Sensitivities Are a Gift From the Divine

Some have a tougher time moving through the feelings associated with a Divine message more than another psychic being might. Usually someone that picks up on psychic input regularly each day will be used to it, regardless if it's intense. If you watch the same scary movie repeatedly, then you jump less at the scare parts than you had done when you first watched the film.

Part of being emotionally sensitive and in tune means developing emotional detachment. This takes practice where you are spending time working on how you comprehend situations around you and learning to not take much if anything personally. It's re-training your mind on how it perceives circumstances whether in the physical or spirit worlds. This can be difficult for a sensitive, an empath, someone ridden with anxiety, or a Clairsentient, because it's their overall nature to feel the intense psychic input, the messages and guidance coming in, as well as other people's energies.

As a clear sentient being, your goal is to gradually learn to not enter particular situations that you know will negatively tamper with your psyche. This includes avoiding locations you know will be crowded. You won't go to the mall or a grocery store in the middle of the day on a weekend. I have a Clairsentient friend who doesn't go outside until nighttime when most people are back indoors again. Although, in general he's a night owl and doesn't mind, but has said that he waits for people to go back inside so he can go outside without interference. There are occasions where this is an annoyance, but there is no wiser alternative that efficiently aligns with his equilibrium.

Whenever you arrive somewhere and see a crowd of people and feel dread or anxiety every single time, then this is a sign that you have strong Clairsentience. The extreme side of this fear manifests into social anxiety and/or agoraphobia, which can affect anyone regardless if you're shy or highly sociable.

I've come across people on both sides of the spectrum from the introverted to the extroverted that have Clairsentience. It's less shocking to find an introverted person who has social anxiety or is agoraphobic, but there are also extroverted people who crave constant social stimulation and are outgoing, but are also exceptionally sensitive that it keeps them tied to the home base unable to be out in crowds let alone outside period. They have a harder time because part of their outgoing nature desires constant people engagement, yet the sensitive part of them causes them to take caution and retreat.

The psychic input coming in from Heaven doesn't bother me no matter how intense it is. This is because the input is usually surrounded with a layer of love. It's other people's energies that bother me, so I can't be around that no matter how desperately someone might want me to. I call on Archangel Michael to shield my soul with a layer of white holy light if I need to enter a nest of toxic energies on any given occasion.

Sometimes you can do everything possible to not be affected by psychic input and yet you're still affected. Mediums and psychics become used to the input over the course of their lifetime that they become less bothered by it, but it can still happen even for those who practice emotional detachment. There are times where I am jarred by the psychic input coming in, but it's a temporary jarring, and then it rolls off naturally on its own. It's not something I'm consciously aware I'm doing. If it's extreme, it can take its toll on me energetically. In a sense, one can say it comes with the territory. Requesting regular assistance from Heaven helps ease the feelings. That means you ask them to shield you from this kind of dark energy daily.

Paying Attention to your Sensitivity

As a sensitive, you may find a tendency to take things darted at or around you personally. You might negatively react in ways that is disproportionate to the circumstance taking place. This is the case even if it doesn't feel that way. It is only in hindsight when you look back do you realize that there was something else going on with your feelings and state of mind that caused a larger reaction. It can a challenge to decipher if what you're picking up on is a message from the Divine or from your ego. This challenge can span a lifetime as you learn to differentiate between all input you're picking up on.

The good news is that because you're a sensitive, you

are more in tune to the vibrations around you than others might be. It's just a matter of honing in on what is Heavenly guidance and what is not. The other plus is that if you're highly sensitive emotionally, then Clairsentience (clear feeling) is one of your stronger psychic clairs. This is where you feel the messages and guidance coming in from spirit. You are learning to distinguish between what is a Divine message and what is your lower-self yanking on the reigns. Your lower-self is the space the darkness of your ego enjoys controlling and bringing out to cause chaos and turmoil.

Learn to have a stronger relationship connection with your feelings, so that you can detect if an uneasy emotion is a psychic hit and heavenly guidance, a reaction from your ego, or a side effect from something you've ingested into your body. Too much caffeine can make you anxious and more stressed. Too much alcohol can cause you to feel erratic, angry, unsettled, or depressed. Some toxins you ingest can create artificial emotions that give the illusion that you're connected with spirit, when in truth you're connecting with your ego. Consuming toxins in large quantities can cause this deception, but again this is not condemning or judging anyone that indulges in it. I have an extended family that enjoys their alcohol and weed and there is no judgment. This is about being aware of what can cause some of the turmoil or disconnectedness with spirit. Keeping certain toxic guilty pleasures in check, balanced, and in moderation is harmless, but of course abstaining as much as possible is even better. You know what your guilty pleasures or vices are and whether or not it's hampering or enhancing your life in positive ways.

Being sensitive is a blessing from the Divine. You might not feel like it is when you're sensing every nuance within and around you, including the uncomfortable stuff. Pay attention to those sensations to determine whether it's your ego or Heaven relaying messages through your Clairsentient feeling sense. They could be guiding you to make lifestyle adjustments that continuously cause you turmoil. If the same person around you keeps instigating grief and upset, then what can you do to change that? If you've found a friend has pushed themselves into your life who you don't care for all that much, then what can you do about it? The immediate action step is to begin the process of dissolving them from your life, or keep them at super low doses if you're not prepared for complete elimination. Sometimes it's not that simple if it's a spouse, parent, sibling, or close family member.

Think of you and your comfort before any other. It's not selfish to make sure you are taken care of first. Only when you're taken care of can you focus on others. Boundaries need to be set in your life where you are strict and disciplined about who and what you invite into your soul's auric home. These systematic restrictions also include what you're putting into your body.

What are you consuming that soon causes you to feel worse than you did before you consumed it? Sometimes the side effects are worse than the disease. Pay attention to what ultimately aggravates you and brings up negative feelings. You're more than likely a super sensitive being, so something will negatively affect your welfare more than it might with someone who is less sensitive. This includes who you surround yourself with, what you consume, and what you read, such as gossip or certain negative media. If your emotions are provoked into negativity whenever you read about the same topic, then stop seeking it out and reading it. Stop ingesting something that worsens your emotional state. Extricate someone out of your life that never brings anything positive to your world.

Pay attention to what you consume. If you're addicted to numerous daily energy drinks and you're always edgy and irritable, then it's time to dissolve or reduce the intake of this toxin. Seek out healthier alternatives that can help give you energy and focus without the side effects.

If you find you reach for a beer or a glass of wine after work everyday and part of you desires to stop or it winds up making you feel worse, then rotate the days where you substitute the alcoholic drink one day and the next day you sit outside with a calming tea such as chamomile, lavender, or tension tamer tea.

Guilt feelings over anything will lower the soul's vibration, and this includes feeling guilty over having a beer. If you're going to have the beer, then have it without guilt. The guilt emotions will reveal a drop in your vibration.

Three separate people take the same alternative herbal supplement only to discover they all had a different experience with it. Some had a positive experience, while another had negative side effects, and the third participant felt no noticeable change.

Someone says, "I have two beers and I don't feel much."

While another says, "I have one beer and I'm on the floor."

Everyone's physical chemistry is different from one another. What works for one person might not work for someone else. This is about knowing and understanding what you can safely handle by gauging the effects beforehand, during, and afterwards. This is all aligned with paying attention to everything within and around you. Awaken your extra sensory perception in all aspects of your life so that you may grow even more aware than you ever have.

Trust Your Divine Instincts

Tune in and follow the guidance and leadership of God, Spirit, or Divine. Avoid allowing your purpose to be taken away by other people. They may not have malice by wanting you to follow them and do what they want you to do, but if that means it's going to take you down a path that is disagreeable to your soul, then you are going against your integrity and the repetitive warnings from your Spirit team that something is off. Spirit doesn't give you guidance and messages for their sake. They do it for your own protection and higher self's soul purpose. They can see what's coming up ahead even when you don't. You're not here to live other people's lives.

There may be times when you lose someone close to you by choosing not to do something that feels unfavorable to your heart. Your Spirit team has greater things in store for you beyond being held back by others. Avoid falling into the toxic allure of people pleasing. As a sensitive, you may be more caring and wanting to help out, but if something feels off about what you're being asked to do, then trust that instinct.

Generally, the first sense I receive about anything is more often than not a psychic hit communicating something important that ends up coming to fruition. My personal guidance system comes from above, and not from other people, and so should yours. Your sensitivity is a gift to help you make the best decisions or course of action while on your life path, even if it's not what someone else wants you to do.

In the next chapter, we'll take a look at some of the ways to communicate with your Spirit team, in order to help you make sounder decisions in life.

CHAPTER FIVE

Communicating with the Divine

No spirit being in Heaven can interfere with someone's free will choice unless they are specifically requested to by that soul, or if the decision the soul is making will result in their premature death. Heaven sits back and watches human souls paint themselves into a corner hoping a rush of clarity will seep in. This is why you must formerly request Spirit intervention, guidance, and assistance. When you invite any spirit in Heaven to step in, then your life becomes a bit easier than if you didn't ask for Divine assistance. Challenges are inevitable on Earth, but moving through those challenges more swiftly helps when you have your Spirit team on your side.

Connecting With Your Spirit Team

Pushing for an answer from the Divine will block the ability to pick up on incoming messages and guidance. Anything connected to fear will sever the connection line. Psychic communication hits filter in when you're in a calm non-judgmental uplifting state. You let go of any resistance while avoiding the desire to push for an answer. Work on regular vibration raising exercises that include clearing your mind, body, and soul of any toxic debris. This can be done in meditation or stillness, as well as through the elimination of vices that you know are holding you back from achieving.

Sit or stand in silence releasing intrusive toxic thoughts and feelings until you are a clear vessel to absorb Divine input. Seeing or hearing celestial wisdom clearly is restricted if you're constantly listening to or paying attention to the noise around you. The noise is everybody else, the media, your negative thoughts and feelings, and the physical concrete world sounds. Physical world sounds are things like car noises, airplanes, and crowd chatter. This doesn't include the sounds of the ocean waves crashing and hitting the sand, or the wind blowing against the side of a mountain. Turn the obtrusive physical sounds all off if you want to truly hear God.

Find a quiet place to sit and be still in prayer or meditation. Allow your Spirit team to know what's bothering you and what it is that you would like help with. If you can get out into a nature locale, then this is ideal, whether it's your backyard or a park, somewhere you can be alone in God's paradise to release. Take continuous deep breaths in and release it all, because you don't need to carry that harsh energy around.

When you feel defensive, emotionally hurt, full of anger, depressed, then Spirit always advises you to get out in nature. The word nature needs to be emphasized because going outdoors to a crowded mall is not what is going to center you. Find balance in those instances and detoxify your soul and body.

Open up the space around you to bring in your Spirit team. You can do this through meditation or quiet time. Play uplifting powerful spiritual background music, light candles, incense, or whatever you choose to bring you and your soul into a centered space. Be patient, give it time, and call them in.

If you pull cards to help with the connection, you can't pull cards quickly and assume the guides are there. Call them in and give them time to come in. Don't control what you hope the answer will be, but allow it to flow in when you're in an emotionally detached space. Release any unforgiveness in your heart about yourself or others. Let it go by visualizing it moving out of you and upward towards Heaven for transmutation, so the weight of that toxin is released.

Paying attention to the messages and guidance coming in from your Spirit team can help you navigate through your Earthly life much more swiftly. They can help you recognize when something is intended to end, or when you're to take action on a circumstance, and so on. They can help when you learn to pay attention and recognize those hits. No one can do that for you. You may go to a psychic reader for answers, but may not always get the messages you seek. This is because in the end it is up to you to decide how your life is going to go and what decision you are to make. You're not a puppet on strings that can be controlled by another being.

An impeccable psychic reader, healer, and counselor can give you clarity and direction, but it is up to you to make the ultimate decision as to the best option. It is up to you to make that decision for your life. It is your life and you are the manager and CEO of it. This is the same way an extraordinary CEO at a company will hear other input or ideas from the employees, but ultimately it will be the CEO's decision as to the best course of action. This is the same way you manage your life. You may bounce ideas off as to what you should do about something with other people. You'll take that into account, and mull it around in your mind, ask your Spirit team for guidance on what to do, then eventually make the decision based on where you're getting the strongest vibrational pull.

You can minimize the difficulties in your life when you ask for heavenly help and guidance, and then tune in to that still place within where these answers reside. You don't need someone else to give you confirmation, because you have the confirmation.

Take a deep breath in, and focus on centering yourself, elevating your faith, and stripping away any fear based thoughts that get in the way of preventing blessings from falling into your vicinity. You are not alone or being ignored even when if it sometimes feels that way. Allow any negative toxicity around you to dissolve away. This will crank up the volume of the angels, and then God comes flowing in effortlessly.

If the answer is not present at that moment, then give it time. Pay attention as you move forward in life for the answer. Sometimes the answer doesn't come in right away when you ask for it. It can come in at a later date. It can be days, weeks, months, and even years later. Although, the latter is rare, the years later is typically when the event you're asking about isn't going to take place until further into the future. Because it's so far out, you're unable to psychically pick up on it. It's only as you grow closer to the date does the information begin to become clearer and stronger without breaking away from that energy vibration.

Be granted the wisdom to understand why events

beyond your control take place. Let God and the angels be your driver when it feels as if you have no more strength to persevere. They will re-charge and re-ignite your soul when you request it. Talk to God and your Spirit team daily and pour your heart out. You are heard whether you believe you are or not. You can communicate your request with your thoughts, in prayer, out loud, and in writing. It doesn't matter how you communicate, but that you do.

What's been on your mind lately causing you inner turmoil? This is a clue as to what you need to let go of. Have the intention of letting go of it and releasing it to Heaven for positive transformation. Unhappiness in any area of your life is also a way to discover what it is you need to change. Have you forever been unhappy with your job? What action steps are you comfortable with making to change this? Pour your heart out to your God and your Spirit team.

Write to your Spirit Team

One highly effective way of communicating with your Spirit team is through writing. When you communicate with any higher being in Heaven, you are communicating with God by default since they are extensions of him.

When you sit down to write out what you'd like to say to those on the other side, there is a stronger intention and force behind it. This force intention is energy that carries solid weight. You find your intention to be stronger with your thoughts, while someone else prefers to say it out loud.

I communicate using the various ways one can communicate, but I've found it efficient when I write it out. Part of this is because I'm a writer and it's easier for me to communicate through the written word. I'll sit down and open a new email message box and address it as you would with anyone. "Dear...."

I'm notorious for emailing myself hundreds of letters to God, my Spirit team, and myself.

You can write a letter to a departed loved one who you miss dearly, because they can read what you are writing when you grant them permission. The addressing of the letter is granting them permission to read it. When you request heavenly support or guidance, you are heard the instant you call out to them. It doesn't matter if the request is big or small, because you are heard regardless. You cannot get away with a lie in Heaven the way you can with others on the planet. You might write or say one thing, but what's in your heart is what's heard and understood to be the real truth by any spirit being in Heaven.

Sometimes when you're in a discombobulated state, it's easier to sit down and write it out in an email, on a notepad, or wherever you usually write. I email my letters to God and Spirit team to myself and file it away in a folder marked, "Angels". This is where thousands of letters and private communications with my team live.

Writing instead of speaking or thinking the words can help you articulate it more efficiently. It forces you to stop for a moment and type out what you're experiencing. This is also therapeutic giving you a sense of calm. Any sudden feeling of serenity is the angels easing the stress you're feeling as you write it out. You've also moved into a state of stillness, which helps them to get to work on you easier when you're less erratic or restless. It can also help you make sense of the words you're putting out into the Universe.

As a writer, I find writing assists with bringing on clarity and focus, but not everyone is comfortable with writing something out. I have friends who are naturally sociable verbally and prefer to speak the words rather than write them out. These are the gifted speakers that dominate through voice, rather than the pen.

One friend has said in the past repeatedly, "I talk. You write."

Those friends tend to leave me long voice messages that cut them off, as there is no more space. They have to call back and continue in another voice box. There are times I call them to say, "I want to talk about this, but I'm going to write you first, then we'll discuss it."

Everyone has different ways of communicating from one another that dominate. This is the same way all souls have varying psychic gifts from one another that also govern. In the end, it doesn't matter how you communicate with Heaven, but that you do.

Pray Instead of Worry

Challenges can be easier to move through when you pray and ask for daily help and guidance. This must also be followed up with you paying attention to the repetitive guidance coming in, then you take action on that guidance. Often when you ask for help in prayer you will be guided to take action on something to help it along. Pay attention to the recurring guidance asking you to take action on something. It will continue to come into your aura indefinitely until you do it. This taking action step will never ask you to harm, hurt, or hate anyone including yourself.

Prayer is intended to help you move away from worry and fear. You invalidate a prayer when you continue to worry afterwards. The worry tells Spirit that you don't trust their intervention and assistance and so you will continue to worry as a backup plan in case God doesn't come through. When you receive repeated nudges after the prayer to take action on something, then take action.

Worry is a negative based emotion that makes you believe that something is not going to go according to plan. Sometimes that can create a self-fulfilling prophecy and push what you desire further away from you. You want to ensure that your thoughts and feelings remain positive that you will obtain what you desire.

Most don't favor constant change as it disrupts the momentum they've become comfortable in. All human beings are equal in the end regardless of what they look like, where they are from, or what lifestyle choices they make. No one is better than anyone else even though each of the ego's attempts to scream the loudest to let others know their way and opinion is the best route. In the end, all the world hears is noise. There is no Divine energy light that exists anywhere within that noise.

Others choose not to believe in a higher power when their prayers have gone unanswered. I've had my own share of roadblocks, but there are numerous unseen reasons as to why prayers go unanswered. When it's a human souls time to pass on, praying can alleviate any hardship for that soul crossing over, but it won't necessarily stop them from passing on, because eventually souls will pass on. That soul might have agreed to pass on during that time in that way for a lesson they chose to learn.

There are various reasons that Heavenly requests are not always fulfilled. Sometimes what you're requesting isn't aligned with your higher self and may cause unseen harm or turmoil. Other times there are pieces to the puzzle that need to be adjusted before something can come to fruition. They may also have something better in mind that you're not seeing. One of the other reasons is you're being guided to take specific action steps to help something come along, but you're not pursuing it. Follow the repetitive guidance and messages you're receiving by taking action with the steps you're given.

You're wrestling with an issue, so you request heavenly intervention and assistance mentally or out loud in a prayer. It feels rushed or forced and your ego gets in the way convincing you that no one can understand or hear you from above. You are heard regardless of your state of being at that moment and whether or not you believe your request for help sounds messed up or garbled. With intention simply saying, "Heaven help!" has already formed the connection.

Observe humility, appreciation, and gratefulness. When you experience testy times, it doesn't help when your focus is on the drama swirling around you. When you shift that energy into something positive, the drama grows less hostile as your higher self rises back up and takes charge. Be appreciative for the good you have in your life now. This is shifting negative complaining words and thoughts into something positive. What you're thinking and feeling now is what dictates the direction of how your life will go in the coming months. Sometimes you can get caught up in what you don't have instead of the good that you do have.

In prayer, learn to use the phrase, "Thank you."

When your desires come to fruition remember to say, "Thank you."

It's easy to get caught up in the good that comes in. This is where you ignore where these blessings are coming from. The feeling behind being grateful is a high vibration energy, which attracts in more of the same. Gratitude goes a long way towards manifesting higher feeling experiences.

Tuning Into Divine Messages

The clearest way of knowing if it's a Divine message or not is if it ends up coming true. The other ways are it's felt with a layer of uplifting love around it even when it's a warning. This may seem like common sense, but you would be surprised that the obvious answer is not what is generally thought of or known to be the one. Some believe that psychic input must be complicated and difficult to distinguish, but the truth is ones Guides and Angels do their best to try and convey it to you as simply as possible. When that tap on the head to pay attention to something doesn't work, then they try other ways such as throwing up repeated symbols and signs to get you to notice it. If God has been knocking on your door for some time, then take the hint and open it and let Him in.

A Divine message continuously comes in until you pick up on the repetitive theme happening. This prompts you to take notice and focus on it. It will continue to come in periodically as it pushes you to action. Take steps towards making something happen if that's the gut hunch you keep receiving. The voice of the ego will cause some form of sabotage even if it's minor, whereas Heavenly messages will never cause drama or harm to you or anyone else around you. A Divine message brings good, positive, high vibrational feelings to you or another person.

When it feels like your connection with Spirit is non-existent where you're not picking up on anything, then that's typically a sign that you're too weighed down or distracted by physical and external matters or desires. If you're experiencing any form of negativity whether in emotions or thought processes, then that's a block. Being mired in any of kind of physical distraction will temporarily dim or cut off the communication line with the other side. It makes it seem as if you're not picking up on anything or you're being ignored, which is never true because Spirit is always communicating with you regardless if you can hear them or not.

The Spirit communication gradually opens when you start releasing and letting go of unnecessary toxic distractions, as well as negative feelings and thoughts. If you're not hearing messages or guidance, then examine your life and make note of what's bothering you or distracting you in the physical world. Work on acknowledging it, releasing it, then letting it go.

The answer as to what is creating the block is usually right in front of you. If you have more than one issue bothering you, then you have to let it all go one by one in order to allow the communication to come rushing in. Lifestyle shifts and changes will need to be made in areas where you are able to make them. Some changes you'll be able to make right away, while others will be more challenging, or it will take longer depending on what it is.

Seeking Psychic Input From Others

When one thinks of psychics, they immediately connect that to someone being able to predict your future. Your future is set based on your soul contract coupled with your free will choices. You are creating and designing your own future. Do you need someone to tell you when you'll meet your next soul partner? Or when you'll move into a new home or get that new job? Avoid getting stuck in the cycle of waiting around for something to transpire. Be proactive in making what you want happen.

You might go to an intuitive friend or a psychic to help give you the messages and guidance you seek that you're unclear on, but it's up to you to come to the answer on your own time. Jumping ahead to get the answer instead of doing the work by moving through the troubling experience can be met with disappointment or confusion.

I've heard or read from others that a psychic reading they had was inaccurate or didn't give them the information they sought out. While others may say that it helped give them peace of mind, but only time will tell if it ends up coming to fruition. If the reading helped give you a lift, then its job and intention were beneficial. Sometimes talking it out with someone or receiving an objective point of view from someone who cares can help immensely.

When your life is not where you want it to be, then you seek out a psychic reader hoping to give you some good news. It's rare that one will go to a reader when they're currently on cloud nine on all physical aspects of their life from career, love, finances, health, and home. If you go to a poor psychic, then you can get sucked into the reader giving you false hope. You want to avoid the scam readers. Those might be the ones that overcharge you for their services, or tell you there is a curse around you that only they can lift if you pay them more money. Avoid readers that consistently try to get you to purchase more stuff from them. Those who are where they want to be will go to a reader if they love the craft or desire some fun uplifting soul affirming guidance, since everyone is a work in progress. There are endless stories of people who have a great career, tons of money, and a beautiful love relationship, yet they still feel unhappy inside or spiritually bankrupt. This only further cements that true authentic happiness starts from within the core of your soul, then you expand that allowing it to work its way outwardly.

Noticing Divinely Guided Synchronicities

Notice the little synchronicities placed in front of you that lead to what you're intended to take action on next. Bumping into the same person repeatedly is no accident. This doesn't necessarily mean colleagues where it's expected that you would naturally be bumping into them daily, but it does mean that person you continuously bump into in passing on a beach, while shopping, at a park, on the sidewalk, at a coffee and tea shop, at the gym, and so on. Consider if that person continues to notice you with a mutual glimmer in their eye as if to positively acknowledge you in a way they don't seem to be doing with anyone else around. Maybe it's a new friendship, a love relationship, or acquaintance soul mate intended to relay a message to you that positively enlightens or shifts the direction on your path. Perhaps it's a new business networking connection, or maybe it's the next long term love relationship. Be open to the signs and symbols floating around your auric world that come through as messages from other people. Sometimes these other people are not initially aware they are messengers. They too are picking up on the guidance and messages from their own Spirit team.

While driving one morning, I was listening to a popular open-minded preacher in an earpiece. At the same time on my car stereo I had rock music playing low, which I could hear in my left ear that was open to hear external sounds. The preacher pulled out a verse and said the number "seventeen". At the same time the rock singer on the stereo sang the word, "seventeen". The synchronous way that the number seventeen was said at the same time alerted me to pay attention to it. This is one example in how these signs and symbols sift in front of you to take notice.

When I mentioned this was an open-minded preacher, it

wasn't to be confused with those hate filled vengeance preacher's that cast judgment on people, which I would never absorb or listen to. This preacher focuses on love never uttering a hate filled word before. The good ones are out there when you search for them.

Endings and New Beginnings

Your Spirit team guides you down the best path for your highest self. They'll send signals of warning when you're in danger or if you're insisting on going down a road that's less desirable. If something doesn't work out, then look at that as a blessing where it didn't happen for a reason. There could've been hidden dangers that you were not noticing or paying attention to.

Let's say you or someone you know is going to meet a potential date with someone new you haven't met before. You find you have to push yourself to meet up with this person, or you feel unexcited with challenging feelings around that, then this is a clue not to go. I know that might sound like common sense, but when you're in the throes of a decision like that you'd be surprised to find the ego isn't paying attention to the best course of action. You're wrestling with indecisiveness about it. Unless you're filled with excitement, then don't waste your time or the other persons. Some have found they would ignore that guidance, go on the meeting only to realize immediately that it's going to be disastrous or a waste of time. As you're driving back home you're thinking, "Why did I go? I knew it was a mistake beforehand."

If an ex-lover is moving out of the country, the state, or far away from you, then look at that in a positive way. If you're single, the angels could be moving this person away from you so that you are open to a new person who is more aligned with who you are today. You may think you've been ready and had moved on, but Spirit can see the residual ex energy still lingering in your aura. They have to get rid of this ex physically so that this new person they want to bring you can come in.

This same concept applies to anyone intended to come in, including friendships, acquaintances, or new business connections. At the time it's happening you might be filled with sadness or grief not wanting this ex to leave, but as time goes on and new brighter circumstances come into your life, you realize why this person had to be sent away. You had outgrown them, but didn't know it because they were still hanging around. It was only after they left that you discover your time with them had long come to a close. That person's essence in your life was holding you back from these other brighter experiences screaming to get in, even if you disagree with that notion at the time. Only in hindsight after time has passed do you start to realize the changes that took place after they left. Sometimes this person is drawn away because they have personal soul lessons they need to learn. Other times it's Heaven's way of helping you become less dependent on someone else and start relying on you. You can't do that when this other person is still hanging around.

Life is full of beginnings and endings, doors closing and windows opening. This kind of drastic change can bring on all sorts of emotions from excitement to fear depending on whether or not the change is purposely done at your own hands or if it was the Universe that was shutting the door on things you weren't ready to part with. Understand that when that happens it is happening for a reason, even if that reason is not yet evident. One of the many ways to change and grow is to change. This gets you out of any stuck energy like a rut or stagnancy. This way you can move onto brighter pastures and circumstances.

CHAPTER SIX

Psychic Abilities Are Built Into All Souls

All babies born should immediately be handed a guidebook that will help them navigate through an Earthly life with no problem. This includes knowing to trust and call upon God and their angels while moving along their journey. Perhaps one could assume that every parent, guardian, and teacher would pass on this knowledge, but unfortunately that is not the case. Human beings in general are imperfect, even though their soul is perfection. They are learning along the way, otherwise they wouldn't need to be here. Many do not believe in Guides and Angels, an afterlife, God, or spirit beings. While some believe in the possibility, others believe it's forbidden, some are unsure, and the rest flatly believe in nothing. They believe that when you die, you die, the end.

All souls are privy to the knowledge of being surrounded by at least one guide and one angel before being born into a human body. Throughout the developmental phase in the first number of years as a child, and through the numerous physical experiences, it is inevitable that memory loss occurs where you suppress soul recollections due to physical Earthly life blocks. The information never goes away, but is stored and accessible at some point in your life. It may come through in sweeping chunks or sporadic snapshots. Blocks are formed as the baby moves into childhood and beyond. By the time it reaches adulthood, you may be completely blocked causing complete amnesia oblivion unaware of worlds beyond Earth. There are a great many souls coming into an Earthly life again who are learning to bring that part of themselves back.

There was once a time in Earth's history when we didn't have the foods, drinks, and negative emotional stresses that we have now. We weren't preoccupied by all of the physical material based distractions. We spent more time outdoors and in nature, and the connections were clearer then. At the same time, more people are growing mindful of how these things negatively affect them. They are experimenting with natural herbs and remedies to find the right products that help bring a greater sense of calm focused clarity.

Calm focused clarity is a state that so many are trying to achieve, but have fallen short of due to the break your back work mentality that many nations have adopted. The current work life state is to work you to death until you drop or retire, then you've got a few good years to enjoy it far beyond your prime. This isn't about having an enormous time off to do nothing, which is one extreme where you risk falling into sloth mode, as discussed in my earlier book, *The Seven Deadly Sins*. The opposite extreme is working more than you have time off when it should be equally balanced. Balance your life in all areas where possible to achieve a greater sense of joy and peace. Avoid feeling guilty about the time off you do take for yourself, because guilt is another deadly sin that creates a spirit psychic block.

Being psychic is not a special power or gift, but an extrasensory ability that every soul is born with regardless of their personal human beliefs. This ability is similar to how a human being is born breathing to stay alive. It's a necessity and a part of the soul's make-up the way the human body has organs to physically survive. Everyone has some measure of psychic capabilities that vary from one person to the next, but no one is all knowing and powerful. The soul consciousness has the competence to receive shreds of second-sighted information, flashes of insight, and sporadic foresight, some of which needs to be deciphered and pieced together by you.

Get Out Into Nature to Access Divine Spirit

Every soul on the planet has picked up on psychic hits at some point in their life, even the non-believers and those unaware they were exhibiting psychic phenomena in that instance. Going out into any nature setting with no physical distractions are where the psychic frequencies are highest. It's where God placed humankind long before structures, buildings, and technology dominated. While there are endless benefits to these luxuries, they also play a hand at dimming and blocking spiritual communication. Getting back outdoors can assist in raising your vibration where higher psychic input resides.

Mother Nature is the perfect place for spiritual and personal enrichment of the body and soul. Spirit energy is heavy in those areas specifically because many higher spirit beings do not hang around areas bathed in negativity. They're not drawn to places like big cities, or wherever it's crowded, buildings sandwiched together, or manmade creations. This is because loving spirits are drawn to light and there is little soul light that exists in physical dwellings. There are more angels and spirits watching over every flower, every grass, rock, mountain terrain than anywhere else in the world. Many nature locales contain powerful spirits hanging around those spaces.

The Native Americans were spiritual people, and America was a spiritual land at its conception. This was until it was plagued by puritanical chaotic materialistic greed filled nonsense energy that exists in the country in modern age. The spiritual part of the land sits underneath that debris. The in-tune souls can easily access it when they are centered in grace. They were and are also some of the greatest souls by having finely tuned in Mediumship abilities.

Partaking and Practicing Mediumship

Partaking in Mediumship entails raising your vibration to pick up on your Guide and Angel, while your Spirit team lowers their vibration to meet you half way. You are living in the low-density mark, and they reside in the high, so you both meet half way, which is the medium mark.

Contrary to Biblical passages, Mediumship is not of the Devil and it's not a sin, but it can invite in a negative entity. Many human souls are conducting Mediumship without trying or wanting to. They are naturally communicating with spirit or a deceased loved one because it is one of the many gifts human souls are born able to do, regardless if they believe in it or approve of it. It doesn't matter what your ego believes, because spiritual truth is constant.

Practicing Mediumship should be taken with the utmost seriousness due to the dangers of inviting in a negative entity. Negative spirits do exist, but they do not exist in Heaven, which contains the highest love energy possible. They reside in one of the numerous darker layers amidst the various spiritual planes and dimensions. Many of these spirits are stuck roaming about in the Earth plane. They strayed further from the Light avoiding it for fear of what their ego conscious mind imagines it to be. Some of them will assume it's full of judgment and punishment if they had been raised in a human upbringing that cemented that false assumption into their consciousness. Other negative spirits will hang back on the Earth plane to aggravate a human soul by attaching itself to that person. They might do this if the human being is an addict. If the negative spirit was an addict as a human being, then it will want to continue with that addiction after passing on. Therefore, it will coax the human being to use the addiction they had.

Negative spirits can and will make someone's life miserable. If you've been perpetually despondent and there are no mental health reasons for it, and it's not your general disposition, then there could be a negative spirit in the vicinity seeping itself into your aura. Sometimes just by being in the same room as you can it infiltrate your soul. When you reside in permanent fear, then you risk attracting in a negative Earth bound spirit. Fear is what attracts a negative spirit to you as this feeds the negative spirit making it stronger in darkness.

All possibilities outside of that would need to be factored in. You cannot automatically assume it's a negative spirit, which is a deceptive trick the ego enjoys to conjure up to illicit fanfare. You would need to examine your overall state of well-being, if you've had a history of depression and anxiety, or if a life circumstance threw a curve ball at you through the death of a loved one, the loss of a job or relationship, or any other details that cannot be explained away that prompted your disposition to become indefinitely negative.

This is about those who generally have a sunny optimistic disposition, where everything is going great in their life, but one day they wake up and moodiness sets in and they cannot figure out how or why. It never seems to leave as the weeks and months pass. Nothing in that person's life can explain how this suddenly came about. Doctor checkups reveal all to be well, diet was never changed, and no life altering circumstances took place. There could be the possibility of a negative spirit that's attached itself.

One of the easiest ways to get rid of it is to call in God, Jesus Christ, and the Archangel Michael to surround you with protective white light, and to extricate the spirit out of your vicinity and away from you, and take it into Heaven's holy light.

Demonic spirit entities are inhuman and the worst evil imaginable. However, the odds of a demonic spirit being around anybody are slim having only about a 1% chance of appearing, but that's 1% out of 7 billion. The percentage of appearance is raised if you are someone that practices Mediumship, channeling, or psychic readings as that can awake it from slumber. This is why it's crucial that you observe safe practices when it comes to psychic phenomena, including surrounding yourself with white light before you conduct a reading.

More people than ever before have been drawn into spiritual pursuits as well as the psychic phenomena field. This is fantastic pending that it's taken seriously and cautiously. The challenging side to that with so many doing psychic work is there are readers who have negativity surrounding their aura that is spilling out of them. There is indication they've invited a negative spirit feeder into their vicinity without realizing it. As always use caution when you conduct your readings, and be sure to use safe psychic practice by shielding your space regularly and being disciplined about your environment, emotions, and surroundings.

Nailing Down Psychic Input

Every soul is born with psychic capabilities, and no one is more special than anyone else since all have the gift. Some of the human souls that reveal the most spot on psychic input are not professional readers, or may not even believe in it, but might be open to it. This is that friend who always seems to say things that later come true. It's a repetitive process that many around them notice. They're not doing anything in particular or trying to conduct a reading. They likely don't even know how to read using divination tools. Their body is the tool that brings in the input naturally.

The benefit of having this gift is to be able to make sounder choices in your life, while warning you of danger and what to stay away from. Pay attention to all of your psychic senses and what comes in as you move about your day. Pray for guidance when you feel stuck on an issue and ask for signs on the best choice to make that will not leave you in a challenging state, but will enhance your life.

A political friend asks me, "I know you're not political, but Ossoff or Handel for Georgia?"

I said, "I have no idea what you're saying to me right now."

He clarifies, "That's whose running for the

congressional seat for Georgia. I was curious what you get for them."

I said, "Oh no, I'm not doing that. Besides I've never heard of them or this."

I paused in silence then said, "Handel. Whoever Handel is. That's who gets it."

Hours later he sends me a media link with the text: "Handel won. You were right. Not that it's a surprise."

How do you psychically nail the answer, how does it come to you, or what do I personally do? In this scenario, I didn't do anything. It just rushed in with the snap of a finger like it normally does. There's no special ritual. It comes in, I state it out loud, and then it's confirmed later that it came true. It's the same way I've predicted every U.S. President elect in my adult life. It's either said to me (clairaudience), shown to me (clairvoyance), I just know (claircognizance), or pieces come in through the various psychic channels one after the other, then a year later it ends up coming to fruition.

Any soul on the planet can do that when they're paying attention to the Divine. Sometimes it just pops in out of nowhere. You don't think much of it until later when it's confirmed to be true. The reason it comes in so effortlessly is because you're also not struggling to get an answer. You're just minding your own business going about your day, your vibration is high, then the psychic information slams in. Your ego isn't trying to push for an answer.

It's in hindsight where you go, "Oh, wait a minute, okay that was a hit, but it came in so easily that I didn't recognize it as being guidance at the time."

There are many light workers and warrior of lights threaded around the world working within the political arena to help shift it away from outdated rules that no longer have any benefit in modern times. The political worlds and the people in them have enormous egos. Sometimes their hearts are in the right place, but other times they're operating from a limited space where they are too caught up in it to see clearly. That's the general perception of most of humanity, with the exception being the enlightened ones who see more than the average person. All are capable of becoming enlightened if they refuse to be limited and seek to understand all aspects of human life at the time they are living it.

I had no idea what my politically based friend was talking about and he does that often, but that's only because he's invested in it. Whenever he starts rambling about the current political climate, I have no idea what he's talking about. I still never knew who those two Georgia people running were. I read the headline he sent me with his text after it was confirmed to be true, but I did not read the story, as I don't care to absorb gossip or political media specifically. The other point is that predictions tend to be accurately foretold when you don't have any emotion invested into the question, which obviously, I don't or didn't.

You experience an accurate psychic hit easily in a situation when you don't have emotion invested into it, so your perception is crystal clear without any blocks in the way. You aren't trying to prove anything or find an answer. This is generally how it sifts into your consciousness effortlessly. It's when you are completely emotionally detached from it all.

CHAPTER SEVEN

How Much Does Your Spirit Team Know?

Common questions I hear from others are things such as, "How does one explain horrendous rapes, murders, the torturing of innocent people, etc. Where were those people's guardian angels? You watch an episode of forensic files and it's enough to make you wonder. I wish there was an explanation that makes sense."

It's an understandable concern with an answer that resides in plain view. It's not the job of God, a Spirit Guide, or a Guardian Angel to stop horrific acts from happening at the hands of a human being. Where in any soul contract does it indicate that this is the role they must play? They are guides, which means they guide. A guide is not doing things for you. The human being has free will choice and is choosing to ignore the Divine guidance coming in and doing the harmful act regardless. The majority of people on the planet either do not believe in Guides and Angels, or they are not paying attention to their Spirit team. This goes back to the discussion to watch what you are ingesting in your body and make note of your state of mind, because all of that not only has an effect on your physical body, but it also affects your connection with the Divine. If someone is mentally ill, they are not in their right mind to pick up on the messages and guidance coming in from above to stop any harm they plan on enacting. It's also presumptuous to assume that every shred of living and choices made by humankind can be or will be controlled by God and Spirit, while everyone kicks back and relaxes allowing them to control positive outcomes for you.

In a world plagued with mass shootings or terrorism, notice how a good deal of the events that were targeted were where it's crowded, or they were entertainment venues where alcohol is consumed. Alcohol dims and removes your tuned in connection with the Divine. No one is saying that you shouldn't drink or go to an entertainment establishment. This is something I've frequented and partaken in myself on occasion. The point is being aware that your Divine connection is dimmed to the point that you're not paying attention to your Spirit team's warnings that danger is near, so you need to be hyper vigilante and careful while out. Pay attention to everything and everyone around, while noting where the nearest exit is.

How often after these horrific traumatic events have taken place do you hear about a survivor explaining how they felt something was off before the tragedy, so they left the venue, and then the attack happened? That person was one of the few picking up on the Divine message warnings coming in. Crowded areas in general will create a block with the Divine because you're also picking up on other people's energies that cause psychic interference.

This is partially why I avoid going to crowded places unless necessary or without choice. Many psychics, mediums, and sensitive intuitive empath's have also protested to having trouble going to places that are crowded as it messes with their sensitivities.

The Job of Spirit is to Guide the Soul

I've talked to people who don't want to know the future. Some of the reasoning is due to fearing what might be seen, while others prefer to live life without interference of knowing what's supposed to happen. The other reasoning is some either don't believe in psychic foresight, or the opposite end of the spectrum is because one believes that wanting to know the future is demonic or is against God's law, which neither is true. Although, connecting with the other side can invite unwanted spirits if you're not careful or using protection methods as discussed in the earlier chapter.

Some have stated to being blocked from receiving spirit messages about what's to come for them, but it's not always a block that is the cause. There are answers to questions you're not intended to know either at that time or at all. If you are to know what's coming up ahead with something, then that information would continuously hit you repeatedly and indefinitely until you picked up on it or noticed it.

Spirit can counsel you about certain circumstances, but not if the outcome is also concealed from them too. If it's hidden from them, then it's unknown to you no matter how psychically gifted you are. You're also not intended to know what's coming as it will prevent you from doing the soul work that you need to do that will ultimately bring in what you're hoping will come to be for you. If you knew everything that was coming, then you wouldn't bother doing anything, or putting in any work. You'd sit back and wait, which is a free will choice move that can prevent the outcome from taking place.

The job of a spirit guide is to guide, and not necessarily to inform you about every single detail on your path up ahead. The reasons as to why this is the case is wide and varied. There might be a test you must endure on your own without any handholding. They will not give you the answers to this test even if they are privy to those answers. This is the same way a teacher gives students a test in Earth schools. The teacher isn't going to give the student the answers, otherwise the student won't learn.

Spirit can and may guide you through certain circumstances, and put up warnings or hints if you were straying too far away from where you're supposed to be, but other than that it is up to you to make your own free will life choices. If everything was handed to you the second you asked for it, then you'd become spoiled, would never learn anything, and subsequently would not grow and evolve. When Children are handed everything, then they expect it and will become spoiled throwing a tantrum if they don't get it. The same goes for the soul.

There are certain circumstances preordained or predestined to one degree or another. This includes the many soul mates you cross paths with over the course of your life. Soul contracted circumstances could be missed out due to someone's free will choice. If two souls were intended to come together and unite, but one eventually denies that and moves away due to free will choice, then there is a backup plan where another soul mate will cross paths with you once the guides know for sure that the other soul mate will not be coming back. Spirit can see what's coming down the road towards you even if the soul mate is making poor life choices that prevent the union from happening. Spirit may see that the soul mate will still eventually wrap back around at a later date, but it's taking them longer to make it to you.

Spirit advises you in the areas allowed, while at other times they must remain quiet for your soul's growth benefit. The more open you are, then the more in tune you are to picking up on the guidance they offer. The higher your vibration, and the more in tune you are, then the more you're able to pick up and follow the guidance coming in. When you're in your mind or ego, you may rationalize, overthink, and compute information. When you're in your heart, then you can sense what the Divine is relaying. Your Divine senses will tell you the truth.

If you were intended to know everything that was coming up ahead, then you wouldn't live life. You would instead kick back and do nothing since you already foresee what's coming. Therefore, what's relayed is on a need to know basis through spurts of information. If you're not picking up on anything surrounding an issue, then take that as a clue to continue living life and making sound choices to propel you forward. Spirit will jump in if it's something you're intended to know or that is okay for you to know at that particular time.

This is also the case if you're single and looking for a potential love partner. You may pick up on someone who is coming to you that may have dark hair, so you might stop searching for a potential partner, or you will push away the potential partner if they don't have the characteristics or statistics you were expecting.

The psychic information you received could be incorrect and a fragment of your imagination. It could've been what your ego prefers or your psychic hunch was semi-correct in that there is a person with dark hair coming in, but that's not the partner. That person could be the catalyst that sets up the meeting between you and the actual partner who ends up having light hair. Or the dark haired person could have no connection to a potential partner at all and was simply a friend or acquaintance coming into the vicinity.

In the end, when it comes to the right soul mate connection, then it will happen naturally. There will be no guessing or effort. You will both sense an instant attraction and camaraderie. You will also both take steps to connect mutually and without resistance or strong persuasion. The dance of the lights of both soul mate partners will intertwine effortlessly when they come together.

The Souls Changing Consciousness

Timing is fluid in the spirit world and doesn't coincide with the timing that we know to be time on Earth. Spirit may see something coming soon, in the near future, or out in the distance. When Spirit says, "Coming soon", then that can be anywhere between next month to one year. "Far out in the future" would be beyond that from one year to several years or more. Some factors come into play such as free will choices that you or others make that can bend or extend the event you desire from happening, to when it was soul contracted to take place.

You may have been attracting in the same types of people into your world, or you have had the same types of friendships for years, then one day you go through a major transformation and suddenly you are no longer attracted to the kinds of people you normally were. When this happens, your energy vibration has lifted causing a change on the path you've been on where it's raised and then shifted. You'll know which direction it went in by the kinds of energy that new circumstances end up being based in. When you grow, evolve, change your perception, and work to raise your consciousness, then you can be assured that many of your surrounding connections will change.

I've sifted through so many different levels of energy vibrations over the years that those I hung around with also changed. There are the friendships in my circle that have been around me for decades, because they also personally shifted while being open to the changes I was going through as I with them. Others moved into the acquaintance box where we would remain in touch, but we were not as tight the way we once were on a regular basis. They are good people, which is why we still connect on occasion, but our views and personalities went in different directions.

Life continues on through these interpersonal shifts that move like the tides in the ocean. The soul consciousness is a fascinating energy as it fluctuates, grows, evolves over the course of a lifetime. Then you have other soul consciousness beings on the planet that never grow. They remain exactly at the same intelligence level they were at when born. Those consciousness beings continuously die only to be re-born again in another Earthly life, and so on in hopes of getting that soul consciousness to expand and evolve.

Your current existence might throw you some wild curve balls where you were heading down one path, but then something offsets it and you're suddenly going down another road. This doesn't mean the road is necessarily worse than the one you were already on. Neither were bad roads, but something poignant takes place that upsets the balance and you're re-directed down another path that in hindsight is potentially better than what you previously had in mind.

CHAPTER EIGHT

Blocking Divine Guidance

Having a crystal clear connection with Heaven requires a high vibration. You will know that state has been reached when you feel naturally uplifted, centered, focused, and clear minded. This means naturally and not through artificial substances, which often creates a block even though you're feeling high on life. Anyone buzzed on an alcoholic drink feels great, that's why some drink. It's why I used to drink like a fiend in my early twenties. It was to feel good since feeling good on my own wasn't working.

My Spirit team says the best way to achieve sharper psychic perception is by getting rid of anything humankind made. They understand this is not realistic or practical while having a human experience, but the closest you are to achieving that, then the greater the communication line is.

Witness those who do not need much to survive, such as hermits or gypsies who live in nature solo. They live out in vast reservations of nature where Spirit's connection is strongest. It's positively valuable to take periodic bouts of time out or time off when possible to commune and meditate in nature. Take regular retreats when you can throughout each year. This means taking one to three days off at a time from your busy schedule when possible to vacation in a nature setting. This can be by visiting a beach, desert, ranch, lake, park, forest, or mountain area, unless you already live in a nature region. Avoid taking it for granted, since that can be easy to do until it's gone. Whenever I head down to my beach minutes away, I always feel this wave of feeling so blessed. I'm highly aware this is no accident.

If you're only able to do that one day a month, then that's better than not doing anything at all. Take a friend, your kids, a spouse, a neighbor, an acquaintance, a colleague, or lover if that will help motivate you to go. Sometimes when you make plans with someone else, it's more difficult to back out of it than if you were going alone. Some personalities prefer to go alone to clear the mind with no distractions at all.

Identifying Challenges and Divine Blocks

You wake up one day and realize you suddenly don't like your job or the relationship you're in. Perhaps you no longer feel connected to some of your friends. Dissolving people or tougher circumstances can take time. Someone's job will be the hardest unless you're able to find another job immediately. You don't want to make any drastic reckless decisions such as quitting your job before you have another one. You certainly don't want to leave a love relationship abruptly, especially if it's not abusive in any form. Conversations with your partner should be had in explaining your new found spiritual growth or personal changes you're experiencing that could be altering the dynamic of the relationship. You may even find that your partner is interested in it as well too, or at least accepting of it. Most everything is fixable in a relationship beyond the couple having immensely outgrown one another.

Take a good hard look at your life and examine every shred closely. You won't be able to do that in one day. Throughout different periods each week, your mind will drift towards parts of your life, whether in the present or the past, for you to do a thorough life review. Often the challenges one is having in the present are somehow related or connected to the past. This is whether it was a poor decision made in the past, or a challenging trait gained during your childhood or upbringing. You may not even realize that a traumatic event in your childhood made you gain fear traits that you ended up carrying with you throughout your adult life. It affects your current state today, since the thread is connected to that time in your life. It will continue to be carried with you until acknowledgement over how it started came about, then learning how to shed that part of you, in order to be clear and free of its bindings.

There may be some things you participate in that you will not want to part with, but which are ultimately causing a block in your life. You are your own accurate barometer as to what changes you need to make. If you're unsure, then you'll have to continue living life until it comes to you. Ask for Divine assistance and help as to what needs to be released from your life, then pay attention to the signs coming in from above. This is not necessarily something that you'll come to the realization of in one day. It can be days, weeks, or months before you realize, "Aha! This is it. This is what was in my way. How did I not see this before?"

This is that magnificent moment of enlightenment and clarity. Other times, you may immediately know exactly what it is that needs to be changed in your life, and then you can begin working on removing them.

Sometimes your ego can deceive you into believing that you're not blocked by anything. An example would be the rush you receive from gossip or absorbing negative media that propels you to swim along with it. The rush is deceptive because it's also the same rush high you get from drugs, alcohol, food, or any other toxic vice. A toxic vice can be anything that ultimately contributes to your downfall whether physically, spiritually, mentally, or emotionally.

How about whenever you talk to a particular friend, then your body feels weak and worn out. This is a Clairsentience sign that your vibration has dropped whenever you talk to a friend who is always negative. They might be someone who is always expressing anger, gossip, or complaining. They could be consistently depressed, sad, and down in general without any interest of finding ways to move past that. No particular event makes them that way, but they are always in that state around the clock. This affects you, your vibration, and your overall state, because you are in that energy and you're absorbing it, and becoming one with it.

It's one thing where you offer supportive action oriented words that help this person move past it. It's another thing if they're just agreeing with you, but never taking action steps to correct this. They refuse to admit that their general demeanor has been on the negative side. Acknowledging your repetitive negative state is the same as awareness. Awareness is the first step on the path that leads to recovery.

Some examples of positive lifestyle changes that will raise your vibration are cleaning up your diet, eating healthier, breathing deeper, frequenting nature, and partaking in regular exercise. It is also avoiding large amounts of alcohol, drugs, the media, and people who are toxic, drowning in stress, depression, or poor life choices. This is not to say that you should abandon family members or loved ones who are under stress. There is a fine line between getting too involved that you fall into a dark hole with them, or choosing to remain detached from their drama. You want to avoid being emotionally drawn into someone else's whirlwind of consistent upset, especially on a regular basis. It does nothing to help you and nor will it help by feeding them the same negative vibrational words they're exuding by agreeing with their chaos. This is like sprinkling lighter fluid on a burning fire. This energy expands causing more of that same substance. The hard-gritting practical world places huge heavy burdens on ones back that it cuts off the psychic supply. Finding that healthy balance between both the grounded earth and the spiritual heaven is ideal.

Coffee and Alcohol Psychic Blocks

Your Spirit team is always communicating with you, but if you're not picking up on anything, then notice what you're consuming into your body that can be the culprit. What you ingest plays a part in what blocks the heavenly psychic connection line. This includes the foods and drinks you eat or drink, to the people you hang around with, to your lifestyle choices in general. Notice what feelings you're experiencing as a result of bringing any of this into your aura. If there are any negative based emotions within and around you afterwards, then that will influence the spirit communication line. If your thoughts are negative, judgmental, hyper critical, or full of fear, then that will also affect the psychic input. Everyone reacts differently to certain foods. One person can be fine with having a cup of coffee, while another person will be more sensitive to the stimuli it gives.

Many have asked if coffee and alcohol specifically blocks your psychic abilities. The short answer is yes to a degree for some folks, but the longer answer is that coffee and alcohol in large amounts significantly dims and blocks Divine communication. This is not necessarily the case if you have one cup of coffee, or one or two beers max once in awhile. It's only when you start downing more than that where it can dim the communication line. This overloads your psychic system making it challenging to connect. This is an exercise each person will have to test out to see what works best. Test your connections with a cup of coffee and without one to see where you're most comfortable.

Coffee would also include products with caffeine content in it. Everyone's body chemistry is different where someone can have a cup of coffee or mild caffeine intake and it's not going to completely block the communication line, while others will receive a complete block. It's when you get into super high caffeine amounts causing your stress and anxiety levels to rise. It's the stress and anxiety feelings that dim or blocks the psychic communication line, and not necessarily the cup of coffee or glass of wine.

Not everyone experiences the same effects from caffeine or alcohol though. Someone can have a beer or two max and they find it awakens the connection line with the other side, yet the connection is short lived, because then you start coming down off the high within an hour or two later, and you feel groggy and gross. Your vibration starts to drop and the match between your high vibrational Spirit team grows further away, so with that said the buzz from alcohol is a temporary high like any sort of toxin.

When you get into three glasses of wine, or you're drinking a six-pack of beer, then you're in a drunken state and have no connection. You might pick up on a word or two from God and your Spirit team, but anything coming in is garbled and unclear, or you simply receive nothing but silence. The bottom line is that if you receive silence and hear nothing, then you're experiencing a block. Something you've ingested has created this block, or it can be your emotional state is not on a high vibrational level, even though you might personally feel that you're fine. The clue is the silence you think you're getting from your Spirit team.

You might be under the impression God and your Spirit team is ignoring you, which is never true. It is you who is ignoring them through what you're absorbing into your aura. This is whether through your thoughts and emotions, to your food and drink intake. A drunken state will give you a complete block, partially because your mind is all over the place, scattered, in a fog, and unfocused. Drinking heavy alcohol until you're in a stupor will mess with this clear mindedness and drop your vibration.

This isn't telling anyone to quit drinking coffee, or caffeine, or alcohol, or bad foods, so don't misunderstand this to being a lecture or judgment. It's merely offering what can dim or block the communication line for those concerned. These are basic guidelines that you can take into account or disregard if you choose.

As stated, everyone's physical and emotional state is different from one another. Someone can have a beer or a cup of coffee and still have the connection, while someone else notices that it diminishes. I can have a beer or a glass of wine and pick up Spirit messages, but soon after as I come down or move into the buzzed phase is when I notice the connection begin to dim and sometimes even disappear.

You may find that you love your daily glass of red wine, but one part of you wishes you didn't have that craving. You could decide to reduce the daily glass of red wine to several days a week instead of everyday, then gradually move to once a week, and eventually to once in a blue moon. The once in a blue moon notion is where you can live without it, but once in awhile you share some wine with a friend and you don't beat yourself up over it or feel guilt, since guilt lowers your vibration. You're able to keep it in moderation, but you're not quitting either unless you eventually choose.

It's sometimes easier to eliminate something when you gradually reduce the intake over a period of time, rather than quitting cold turkey. This is because you're slowly and safely allowing yourself and your body to adjust to the new changes you're making. It's not as tough or challenging than if you stopped abruptly one day, which can cause withdrawals and side effects. This applies to anything you're longing to dissolve, reduce, or eliminate. We're just using the coffee and alcohol examples, but switch those words out to the vices you wish to change.

As you were reading those last few paragraphs, you likely already know what it is that has been a concern for you.

Know your body best when it comes to your intake of coffee, alcohol, red meat, dairy, etc. You know what you do that will make you feel a certain way.

None of this should be taken as judgment, as my Spirit team is offering constructive suggestions and guidance to help one's soul improve in certain areas of your life.

This is also not telling anyone that they shouldn't drink alcohol either, which is a common misconception, because we know I love a cold beer at a hot Summer beach BBQ with my Classic Rock music jamming on the player.

Like anything that can be damaging or toxic in large quantities, you want to keep the guilty pleasures in moderation if you have a passion for it to the point where you overindulge regularly to where you wind up face down on the floor all day accomplishing nothing towards building your dreams. This isn't for Spirit's benefit, but for your own well-being. They know that when you are vibrating at a higher level that you are more in tune to the guidance coming in that can help you achieve the dreams you long to conquer. It will also help in giving you more energy and focus to put towards doing other things you love.

I used to drink alcohol like a fiend in my early 20's, then one day as I moved into my mid-to-late 20's, I changed. Those close to me noticed this drastic change.

It led to numerous questions darted my way, "How did you stop? Why did you stop?"

My initial response was, "I was tired of losing a day."

The misunderstanding was that I stopped and went completely abstinent, which is not true. I still have a beer or a glass of wine on rare occasions, but I'm no longer drinking a 6 pack or 2 bottles of wine in one sitting as I would do during my weekly party in a cup days throughout my late teens to early twenties. I felt like crap and would lose a day when I used to do that. I conducted a trial and error process where I discovered what would make me feel uncomfortable and lose my Spirit connection, as to what would strengthen my connection. I spent a great deal of my twenties and thirties keeping all of that to myself, except to my circle of close ones. Eventually, I began sharing little reveals here and there through my writing work for those interested or curious in it. I would dissolve or eliminate certain toxic vices and pay attention if I noticed any spiritual, emotional, or physical difference.

With coffee I discovered that it didn't seem to matter if

I had a cup of coffee or not. This is because I felt the exact same way with or without it, so I would say, "Well, then why am I drinking this everyday? It's not doing anything of any benefit, since I still feel groggy afterwards."

This was my personal choice to do with my Spirit team. I'm not anti-coffee at all, but just no longer crave it anymore. Not that someone might not catch me have a fun coffee drink with a friend on a rare day, but mostly I stick with teas. You don't beat yourself up over breaking your little discipline routine once in awhile. You're not going to go to Hell and nor will you be banished out to pasture for enjoying a guilty pleasure from time to time.

Take note what is a human made substance and what comes from the Earth. Human made substances tend to play a part in dimming the Spirit connection, while anything from the Earth can help enhance it such as fruits and vegetables. In the end, when you don't want to give up what you love or you're not ready, then remember the moderation rule if you're trying to simultaneously have a stronger Divine connection.

If you're going to conduct a psychic, angel, or spirit reading connection for yourself or someone else, then hold off on drinking those two margaritas until you're done. Hold off on eating a large meal as that can weigh you down and will reduce any heavenly communication. It is up to you to decide when you are ready to reduce, dissolve, or eliminate a toxin or block, and then begin that process safely with your Spirit team.

Archangel Raphael the Healing Angel

Archangel Raphael is known as the healing angel. This is because he has performed miraculous healing for physical, emotional and mental issues when others have requested his help. The light that consumes him inside and out is bursting with emerald green light. Whatever he touches with this light begins the process of healing.

Call on Archangel Raphael whenever you are experiencing any issues related to physical, emotional or mental well-being. Visualize his healing green light being showered anywhere that requires attention. Also understand that he may guide you to the answer that can remedy any issue. This may be from being guided to the right medical specialist, or to healing medicinal properties that can assist in a medical related issue.

Raphael works alongside Mother Mary and Jesus Christ during great catastrophes where souls are extricated abruptly leaving them disoriented for a bit. The disorientation is not painful, but more of a confusing amnesia where your soul is not quite sure what's just happened.

I'm a super physically active soul and with that I've faced some physical consequences. One of them included an incident where I felt this sudden pain in my right arm, or what is called the *flexor carpi radialis* muscle in the human forearm. Days passed and the pain still came and gone without any sign of healing. This was when I realized I needed heavenly intervention.

I called in Archangel Raphael before I went to sleep. I rubbed my hands together until I felt the heavy friction between them. I pried my hands slowly apart and I clairvoyantly saw an emerald green light fire bursting between them with energy. I took that light and began hovering one of my hands over the area where the pain is. And it is done.

When I woke up in the middle of the night there were still signs of slight pain here and there, but I headed back to sleep anyway. I woke up the next day and discovered that the pain was gone. I twisted and turned my forearm.

Nothing. No signs of any agitation or anything. Days passed into weeks and I realized that the pain had evaporated and never re-surfaced.

I believe in the power of prayer because I've witnessed and personally experienced countless and endless miracles over the course of my life as a result. When I don't ask for help, then help is not forthcoming. I've always followed and adhered to faith healing combined with medicinal healing. This is by bringing in prayer over an issue, while being guided to medicinal or herbal remedies to assist in bringing the body back to tip top form. Some only believe in faith healing, which has resulted in harm and even death, while others will pop a pill, and not bother to include Divine intervention. Their illness persists for much longer as a result, and sometimes they never get better.

Archangel Gabriel
the Angel of Creative Expression

Removing blockages can be done through body movement and physical exercise. What kind of health issues does one have that prevents them from regular exercise? For some it's...dare we say it, laziness, but for others there are some in this life that are genuinely authentically physically crippled and absolutely cannot. This applies to those who are physically capable of exercise, but just don't want to. Exercise helps in dissolving blocks with the Divine.

Another way to dissolve blocks is through creativity. Dive into creativity, creative pursuits, and projects when you find you're falling into a blockage. You've lost energy, passion, and a zest for life. Creative expression can assist in reopening that pathway to Divinity again. Archangel Gabriel is the one to call on to help with procrastination and in awakening your creative gifts. All Angels and Archangels are genderless and have no anatomy, despite artists depicting them in various physical forms in paintings and art. It is true they may take certain forms in appearing in ways that are recognizable to that person.

Archangel Gabriel has a feminine energy because she assists others by pulling things out from within, whether that is creative expression, passion, nurturing your inner child, mothering Children, pregnancies, or the birth of a project or endeavor. The uncertainty of how Archangel Gabriel is perceived has carried on for many centuries. This goes back to how life was lived during biblical times. Centuries ago the world was a male dominating patriarchal society, and the female form was considered forbidden and secondary. For that matter, the Catholic Church changed Archangel Gabrielle to Archangel Gabriel and demanded that she be seen, depicted, and perceived as a male. The only female deity allowed at that time was Mother Mary and that was because she gave birth to Jesus Christ.

No one can control the free will actions of mankind. This change has caused confusion over the centuries, where some believe Gabriel to be male. The church eventually corrected this perception, but by that time the world was already training one another to continue to see "Gabrielle" as male.

Gabriel is an egoless genderless being unperturbed by the false beliefs of man, since all human souls have free will choice to believe what they want to believe. The "Gabriel" name may have a masculine tone to it, but gender identity is strictly reserved to human souls being taught and trained to separate male and female. This has also caused quite a bit issues among humankind.

Archangels and Angels will appear in a form that the individual is used to in order to be recognizable, even though it is not their natural appearance. They can morph in and out of a light source as a spirit.

It wasn't until the 1900's and beyond when women in some countries were allowed to vote or have an opinion. It was taboo for women to get a divorce or even work. Gender equality didn't really move full steam ahead until beyond the 1970's. In some countries, women are still forced to take a back seat specifically in third world countries. Therefore, it's not surprising to know that during biblical times, man did not want a female deity figure.

Archangel Gabriel is my agent guiding and moving me along my career path since I started the workforce as a teenager. Luke, one of my guides, works along with her on all career work related endeavors. My writing work is done with the both of them present.

Gabriel has clairvoyantly appeared numerous times over the course of my life. Her physical appearance is neither male nor female. The shape of her face is not like a human face, but the structure of it is soft and on the feminine side, almost androgynous. She drops down into my space in a bright copper colored light with white sparkles and wears a light blue cloak that covers everything except for her face. The cloak is dominating and flowing. She also doesn't have wings, even though that's how artists paint her.

When she moves into my space, I clairaudiently hear music rush up emitting out and around her. There is a sudden intoxicating joyous uplifting feeling that soars through me. The lyrics to, "Hark the Herald Angels Sing!" were words that she whispered into the consciousness of the writers of the song. She communicates predominately through me clairaudiently and telepathically. Telepathy is one of the primary ways of communication on the Other Side.

CHAPTER NINE

Stomp Out the Darkness and Master Confidence

A healthy ego is being confident in your abilities and not shying away from announcing it to the Universe. The meek don't get far, so allow the confident part of your soul to come out and shine its light brightly into the ethers. Visualize that light expanding and growing more blinding than you can imagine that it blasts everything away in its wake. This is how powerful your soul light is back home in Heaven. While it may be ferociously beautifully strong on the Other Side, that light is still within your soul. It is simply contained inside the temporary physical body you've inhabited this lifetime. This light can still fluctuate and expand and contract as it does back home while within your body.   It can get crushed under the weight of the Earth's energy density and the darkness of ego, but you have enough power to let the light out in an explosion that it breaks apart this darkness at your own will.

Turn Anger Into Positive Action

The ego can manifest fear into anger. Depending on your overall character and nature, your temperament will be different than another person's. The way you react in anger will vary compared to someone else.   Is the Dalai Lama or the Pope running around bullying people on the sidewalk, verbally attacking people on social media, or starting fist fights for no reason?

All forms of anger are toxic putting stress on your health and body, but that doesn't mean you're supposed to pretend to be happy about someone betraying your love and trust. Even if you pretend that you're fine and put on the false face, then your body, your Spirit team, and God knows how you really feel about it. It's your senses they read and can instantly pick up on that have far greater energy than the pretend face you're putting on for others.

It's what is in your heart that is read, and not how much money you have in the bank, what kind of car you drive, or the awards you have under your name. It is your character and heart the angels see and know to be true.

This is also why you cannot get away with a lie with any spirit being the way you can with another human being, unless of course the human being has a high degree of Claircognizance (clear knowing). Claircognizant beings know when someone is lying, even if they don't call them out on it. Most of the time depending on how severe or harmless the lie is they just keep it to themselves. If everyone observed Claircognizance, then they would be able to detect when a media story is exaggerated or produced with the indirect intention of riling your ego up.

Look at what it is that you continuously jump to anger about. This is one of the many clues as to what your many life purposes are. The next step is to channel that anger positively for the greater good. For example, if you always get angry over those who toss trash everywhere but in a trashcan, then use the anger constructively by seeking out ways to prevent that from happening. Those who get really upset over anyone dumping trash in the ocean might be someone who chooses to join an organization like Greenpeace to fight to keep Earth clean. They are turning their anger into positive action.

Someone cut you off in traffic and you immediately rise to anger, but then depending on who you are, you hopefully get over it within a minute and move on. How about if you discover the person you devoted yourself to in a committed relationship or marriage had been unfaithful to you, or pulled the rug out from underneath you by leaving the connection. The anger felt with that will be greater than the anger over someone cutting you off in traffic. Except in this case the anger turns to sadness and grief.

For others, they'll remain in the epicenter of that anger becoming hardened and indefinitely bitter. You'll develop fear that every potential future relationship will result in that person doing the same thing. In that sense, you continuously create the reality that this is what is to be. It plays out in the exact same way over and over again with future mates until you choose to break the pattern and make character adjustments to prevent the same lessons being repeated indefinitely.

Critical Gossip

Avoid gossiping and negatively talking about others and what you feel they did to you. When you find you're doing that, wrap it up and shift the words to positive action oriented words and how you plan to bring things to a resolve. The same goes for those who criticize you. You will be criticized at some point in your life if you haven't already. This is whether you offer services to the public or someone you know harshly criticizes you in a way that is non-constructive with malice intentions. Many have offered different ways of handling that from examining what they're saying, to engaging with them calmly and positively, to sending them love and light. The best way to handle someone like that is to ignore them. You don't engage with someone who is ranting negatively at or around you. The same way you avoid inviting any negative spirit into your aura. There is no positive benefit at all in doing any of that.

The darkness of ego is the culprit behind negative moods and thoughts. When you allow the light to come cracking in, then that is a sign your higher self is taking back the control. The ego is a dreadful culprit in getting in the physical world's way of true happiness.

Refrain from using world events as a reason to fall into the lower energies of blame, gossiping, and politicizing. Human trauma of any kind can shake one's faith. Don't allow any human tragedy to consume you to the point of fear that you disconnect from the Divine. Free will choice and the darkness of ego have no connection with source.

There will be a natural cycle of uncomfortable emotions that you'll endure, play out, and move through until you've reached that space of having forgiveness for anyone that upset you. This is so you can graduate from that and move forward and onward in your life.

Picking Your Battles

One of the greater challenges many have is maintaining a sense of serenity and peace. This includes getting along with people that are different from you. You're presented with varying circumstances that can easily generate upset. When this happens, then be mindful that it's happening. Your soul was born peaceful and without judgment of those different from you. If someone is happy living their life and they're not hurting anyone, then it's no ego's place to interfere with that. This also doesn't mean you allow someone to bully or run you over. You have to be hyper-vigilant and aware as you navigate Earthly creation whenever other people are around. Many sleepwalk as they travel about their Earthly life. They move through the same daily routine activities they were trained to do by others early on. Some never work to improve, enhance, and awaken their true spirit, but merely go along with the popular fads and lingo of that time period they grew up in.

A lower state of being seems to be easier to attain, than achieving a higher state of being. The irony is most people who are in a low vibrational state wish they had the latter. They find it challenging to reach a higher state of being. When you're angry about something, the last thing on your ego's mind is not about re-centering as quickly as possible. Yet, that is the next step to take when you've fallen into a space of negativity. This isn't asking you to deny your feelings of anger, since anger is one of the many emotions that exist in humankind, but it is an emotion that comes from the ego. You want to find the source of what is causing that anger, then look at the grander picture of what you're angry about to see if it's misplaced or not.

Every hour spent angry is a waste of time. Take that anger and channel it positively through action that can fix or correct whatever it is your angry about, otherwise work on letting it go. Being angry with someone else isn't going to change or enlighten that person. They're off happily doing their thing while you're at home brooding over something they did, said, or anything about them. This can be someone you know personally, a public figure, or a stranger.

Some tend to get angrily riled up over something a public figure said or did in the media. This does nothing to change that person and it doesn't resolve anything. You don't know them and you're not in their house having a conversation with them. Instead your aura marinates in that toxic cesspool energy that doesn't hurt the target. It hurts you and your well-being, while simultaneously blocking heavenly spirit guidance from coming in.

Many fall into that allure by posting repetitive complaints on their social media accounts that ultimately wastes time. This dark energy flows into the cells of your body and gets lodged in there when improperly channeled. If the anger is a daily pattern or left unchecked, then it can manifest into something more harmful such as a breeding ground for future diseases and health issues. When you're in the epicenter of that developed hurricane of toxicity forming in and around you due to your own words, feelings, and thoughts, then it's difficult to be aware that you are. Dark energy blinds you to the truth. When one falls into the deep seed of repetitive anger, they are out of their minds, and oblivious to how far down the rabbit hole they've fallen. They later realize that it's been one thing after another going wrong in their life while being unaware of how or why it grew at such an astronomical rate.

One way to counteract this is by avoiding the gossip media. Stop seeking out salacious top trending headlines designed to attract, entice, and lure you in. The ego loves drama because it's designed to get you caught in its web preventing you from seeking out more positive activities to focus on. Use discernment and good judgment over what is worth knowing and what is something that is out of your hands.

There are a number of people around me who don't get involved in gossip or media to the point that they really don't know what everyone is arguing about, and they like it that way. Unless your job is a position that requires you to correct certain issues you're passionate about, then there is no benefit to joining in with the crowd to argue about the latest dramatic news story. The ones who don't agree with your values won't be positively influenced, so it's a time waster.

Most of the time what people are arguing and gossiping about is forgotten within one to three days as another enticing headline flies to the top of the list to attract in their focus. It can take practice and enormous willpower to not be tempted to read certain types of articles. That practice includes immediately knowing whether something is a gossip piece or is an objective balanced news piece focused on straight neutral reporting. If every time you get riled up over media pieces put up by a particular news source, then it's time to step away from that source for awhile in order to get re-centered and re-directed on more important priorities that will ultimately bring you joy and peace.

The ego part of the soul gets riled up and angry in its own way on occasion. The trick is to catch it when it happens so that you resolve whatever it is that got a rise out of you. Learn to pick your battles and by quickly taking steps to bring that anger back down to the space of contentment again. This isn't about ignoring your anger and your feelings, but like everything connected to spiritual growth and evolvement you're growing more self-aware of the modifications you need to make.

Figuring Life Out As You Go

There is the difference between protesting against something that your values tell you to be wrong, as opposed to rebelling against someone else's sound judgment intended to prevent disaster or chaos from swallowing you up whole. All you can do is let that soul figure it out the hard way. It can no doubt be frustrating because you care about that person and don't want to see them fall off that cliff, but in the end it's not up to you. This is their life and they need to stumble and fall on their own. If you spend all your days doing it for them, then they'll never learn anything. They might learn later in life, or when it's too late long after you've gone. At that point, they have no other choice, but to find their own way solo.

If you're a parent or guardian of a child, then you have some measure of understanding of this. Especially when a child reaches a certain age where they gradually assert their independence and discover who they are as an individual. This means they will rebel even if what you're telling them is helpful. They may purposely defy you and head right for that cliff anyway just to spite you. It can be maddening to see someone you care about walking towards a cliff knowing there is nothing you can say that will stop them from that. The more you attempt to stop them, the more they carry on towards that cliff. The ego is a rebellious beast that will do what it wants, when it wants, thank you very much.

The parent is guiding them not necessarily to be strict, but because they know what will happen if they make an erratic decision. They know because they had gone through it themselves. There comes a point when you need to give someone else wiggle room to be free and discover the art of learning on their own.

A parent is essentially intended to be a guide the way a

spirit guide is for a soul. The guide isn't living the soul's life, but gently pointing them in the direction that will bring in the best result for their higher self. While doing this, they and you ultimately leave the soul free reign to make the choice that sits most comfortably for them, even if it's a choice that will not be desirable in the end. God is much like a parent with all souls hoping to steer the soul away from danger and towards peace.

If a soul doesn't make mistakes, then how can it grow and evolve? Sometimes it can take someone months, years, or decades for the soul to realize that the way they've been doing things hasn't exactly been successful. That's the start of the change potentially happening within them, and then the real work comes in. Many receive the calling from God, but only a small percentage chooses to follow that calling. Receiving the awakened call is just the beginning, because then you have to put in the work.

Stand In Your Own Individual Power

The mind and heart are rarely in agreement with each other. Your heart longs for a particular person, job, or circumstance, but your mind talks you out of it. The rational mind loves to dance with the ego, otherwise known as the dance with the Devil. The ego resides in the mind intent on overriding and dominating the higher self. It will insist on doing what it wants to do regardless of what your heart is saying. The ego doesn't like back talk and will stomp its feet in a tantrum after you give it a challenging response that didn't back it up.

There is a reason circumstances take place beyond your control or current understanding. Life ebbs and flows, nothing stays the same, and not every soul sticks around with you throughout your entire Earthly life. Know yourself and learn to be independent of relying on anyone, except God and your angels for guidance.

None of the world drama that goes on matters in the end because every soul on the planet has a Divine plan attached to their consciousness. This is the case even if you cannot see that while in the moment. It is the responsibility and life quest of that soul to come to the conclusion of what their purpose and plan is on its own. No other being can inform them of what it is.

Some find they've given their power away to others, whether it's a friendship, relationship, or family member. There was a time in my late teens and early twenties when I was living hand to mouth with little to no money, but I pulled myself up and began working to take care of me. An example of giving your power away might be if ones partner takes care of things. This prevents you from being independent. Eventually a time comes where you feel suffocated and stuck wanting to move on, but you're unable to because your partner pays the bills and you haven't had a job in years. This makes you feel even more paralyzed and stuck.

You can get unstuck from giving your power away by taking steps to fix the circumstance. Once you find work and begin making your own money, then you are able to take steps to leaving the person you've given your power away to. This is no different than when you are a young person living under your parent's roof. If you don't want to live in your parent's house forever, then you need to become an independent adult and do something about it. Get a job, make money to survive, and find a place to move to. You can't live life depending on someone to save you since this rarely happens and relationship dynamics do end more today than they have in past history.

CHAPTER TEN

Balancing Healthy Selfishness and Selflessness

No one is ever truly in any kind of danger and all is always well in the end. You have Earthly life challenges that hinder your movement from day to day events such as getting your brakes fixed on your car. Now that's another expense you have to deal with. Other challenges such as figuring out how you're going to get out of work early to make it to your son's baseball game, to wondering if your love mate is cheating on you. You have larger challenges such as the death of a soul close to you leaving you to wonder how you'll continue on. A physical death is not the end as hard as that it is to accept and understand when moving through the grieving process. The soul simply moved onto more magnificent destinies that await it. Earthly life is the most limited restricting destiny that it truly is a soul relief to graduate from it.

Bring Your Soul To Its Natural State of Love and Peace

Coming to the end of the road as you close your Earthly life chapter up, you realize if you hadn't before that it was always intended to be about love. Your soul was born from a source of love and you will die right back into that love. Love is the most powerful energy foundation that exists in all dimensions. The only thing that matters is love. The best way to channel energy positively is to remember all things connected to love. Love is what kills energy like anger, sadness, fear, and worry. Outstretch your arms, release any fears, and fall back into the arms of this love. Allow it to protect and guide you on your Earthly journey.

Bring your soul to that beautiful glorious space of centeredness, serenity, and peace. Ignore any drama swirling around you and view circumstances from an emotionally detached perspective without judgment. Increase your faith through prayer and regular conversations with the Divine, knowing and understanding that you are loved and watched over.

Every day should be the most magical time of the year, but the lack of love on the planet that continues to be prevalent makes it less enchanting. Remember to love and accept others even if their values are differing from yours. This is easier said than done since many have forgotten about the basic concept of what love is. Humanity continues to have a long way to go before every soul on the planet is aware that it's about love.

Treat everyone with kindness and compassion even if they don't share your values. This goes for all sides of the spectrum, as everyone becomes guilty of it at one time or another. It's not okay to treat others badly. It's not okay to abuse the luxuries you've been given as a free will thinking conscious being. It's one thing to defend yourself from someone who has accosted or randomly disrespected you, but it's another to take it upon yourself to harass someone because they're different and not a clone of you. You reach no middle ground when you're that rigid.

The Sin of Mistreatment and Disrespect

The #1 trait that Spirit doesn't like to see is someone mistreating or disrespecting another person in any form. This means a certain amount of decorum and etiquette is something they prize. Mistreatment is considered one of the most distasteful quality traits for God to witness. Sadly that's also the top trait displayed on the planet by humankind around the clock.

There are different shades of mistreatment and disrespect that exist. Someone treated you unkindly, then the natural immediate reaction is to be reactive or defensive, so you lash out in retaliation. There's also that fine line between how far you intend to go with mistreating another person to deciding to limit your reactions to slights on your ego by choosing your battles wisely and selectively.

Some refuse to give respect to those that are mean to them, which is not what Spirit is saying. Decorum and etiquette more or less point to the same thing. This is about exuding class, compassion, and grace, while giving off a certain level of respect towards others. Humanity has a long way to go with that. There are a great deal of tantrums and stomping around angrily when someone doesn't get their way, instead of seeking out the middle ground in meeting others half way. Treat people with kindness and compassion, but defend yourself with assertiveness if someone attacks you.

One hopes that with age comes wisdom. In your

twenties, you're more likely to be angrily reactive over something than a wise one moving into their thirties and beyond. This is because the older you get, whether in human age or soul age, you hopefully learned to incorporate more of the Divinely guided traits of patience, forgiveness, and humility. What can you let go of, get over, and move on from? The risk you run into when not getting over something is when you fall into perpetual antagonism. Not only does that create enormous weight on your spirit, which can cause damage to your health and Divine connection line, but there comes a point when no one is being helped by the repetitive antagonism.

On the one hand Spirit says to teach people how to respect others, but you also can't get swept away in the noise nonsense. The noise nonsense is ranting and raving with everyone else on social media over the top trending story. That kind of disrespect doesn't do anything except add to the drama and noise. The mistreatment and disrespect here in Spirit's case is primarily the one on one kind, even though all forms of mistreatment are unacceptable to them. This can be where someone has overstepped their boundaries or is not displaying appropriate compassionate assertive protocol.

The worst kind of mistreatment is abuse of any kind whether that's physical, emotional, psychological, and so on. This is what irks and pains Spirit to witness, because in the end whatever you're not able to get over doesn't matter in spiritual truth, since you and all of this will one day cease to exist. To God, all that's seen is everyone disrespecting everybody else with no end in sight. That energy is darting all over the place. At that point, there is no valid reason for it, so just stop.

The most spiritual evolved soul is guilty of it too, as every soul on the planet is at one time or another, but they're aware of what Spirit doesn't like to see and wants to see more of. This statement isn't cut and dry as it can go exceptionally in depth when looking at each case. The general consensus for Spirit has always been the same. Treat your neighbor with respect even if you personally disagree with them. That's a rough trait for all to observe, but one to remember to revert to whenever possible.

This is not about taking abuse. This is for those who deliberately and intentionally cause turmoil in others. Disrespect and mistreatment should never be tolerated. If that means you need to rise into Divine warrior mode to stomp that out, then that is what you must do. You have to teach people how to respect you.

In a perfect world, you shouldn't have to teach someone how to respect others, but the reality is there are billions of children on the planet that haven't been taught the basic concept of respect. If it's not there, then you need to move on. This is also about someone who physically, psychologically, emotionally, or verbally assaults you, then they need to be taught the meaning of respect. This isn't through the means of violence. You have to stand up for yourself when possible.

A five-year-old boy was brutally tortured and abused by his parents to the point where he fell into a coma, then passed away. Those parents need to learn the art of respect and compassion for human life. Walking away from something like that is not an option. There are cases where certain behavior needs to be taught and corrected.

Avoiding someone who mistreats or disrespects you is always the first way to go. This is especially the case with online bullies that take it upon themselves to message a stranger through social media to attack them. You don't bother with that kind of nonsense, but block them instead and move on. Flick them off your shoulder like a bee. When one is in situations where that's not feasible or logical, such as a continuously hostile boss, an abusive spouse, or someone you're living with that perpetually antagonizes you, then there is no choice, but to talk to them and train them how to respect you. Otherwise you will end up spending each day under the reigns of abuse, which ultimately causes all sorts of psychological damage that is difficult to repair.

If someone attacks you online, then you ignore that energy, you don't engage with it. You avoid, delete, block, and move on to more important things. If you did something that instigated mistreatment from someone around you, then be conscious of when you did that and take steps to mend or correct it. Sometimes one can unknowingly hurt someone's feelings without realizing that's what may have caused them to be disrespectful towards you. People are complicated beings and learning to discern when a situation warrants how you'll react in kind to a disrespectful person requires your keen intuitive radar. This goes back to the choosing your battles wisely.

Respect and Compassion

The ultimate reason all are here is to love and to learn how to love. You cannot learn that unless you're thrown onto a planet with others who are different from you. Learn to accept others and see someone's personal truth. You're not saying you agree with them, but a way shower illuminates the way by example.

Be the King or Queen of showing respect and compassion to others. These traits are not popular globally. This doesn't mean that if someone abuses or walks all over you that you take it lying down. Pick your battles and use assertiveness over aggressiveness when slighted. The general demeanor to strive for on a regular basis as much as possible is respect and compassion. Being a compassionate loving person is what garners real attention and attraction from others. If that turns someone off, then don't allow them into your auric circle.

The Divine Act of Selflessness

Being entirely selfless is an act that requires no personal gratification, but there is some measure of fulfillment with the act of selflessness. You require unconditional love in a relationship, but unconditional love is to love without conditions. Most everybody has conditions to one an extent or another. This is especially the case in intimate romantic relationships. You hope the person you're with doesn't cheat or isn't abusive. Those are highly reasonable and warranted conditions, but they are conditions. You can get close to unconditional love as much as you can get close to selflessness.

All human beings have both a light and dark ego. The light ego is connected to traits such as having confidence in your abilities, while the dark ego is bogged down in gossip, anger, judgment, or violence. Some dark egos are power addicts. They are much worse than others where a result is desired for individual egotistical advantage. The result can be damaging even if the effect is not in the form of monetary gain. You can still receive a high soaring feeling of emotional satisfaction. Those who are typically giving by nature are not being altruistic for personal pleasure, but for spiritual nourishment. There are various levels of attainment when it comes to altruism.

To be completely selfless is a Divine act possible to achieve. You are made in the likeness of His being. Therefore, you have the capacity of great love and immense selflessness built within you.

I've witnessed others reach that space of being

completely selfless. They've personally done things to help others without the longing for any kind of gain. No gratitude is required in those instances. The selfless soul desires to make sure someone is taken care of without any fanfare or acknowledgment. Because why offer praise for displaying traits that are present in every soul on the planet.

At the same time, many long for some measure of approval from others. Even the most centered person on the planet doesn't mind the occasional validation. This doesn't make them any less insecure, but it does serve as a reminder to them that the work they're doing isn't for nothing. They can more than likely live life without it after a certain point. When you're in your teens and twenties you generally long for more validation and approval than when you age beyond that.

Altruism or selflessness is part of the universal truth, but it's also a God given trait you were born with. It's universal truth only to the extent that humankind decided to make the act of being selfless a virtue. A universal truth is everyone agreeing to make something be of truth at that time in history. This has been altered as humankind progressed onward. Universal truth is subjective, but basic core values are innately built into a soul operating at full capacity with a high vibration at optimum levels. Parts of the consciousness are God given qualities, while other parts are astrological and part of that person's human life upbringing during the crucial developmental years. It's a cocktail of complicated composites within each soul's make up.

Basic God given traits are displayed while in a high vibrational state. High vibrational states are qualities such as love, serenity, peace, confidence, compassion, and selflessness. The angels are egoless and therefore selfless. They require nothing in return for being selfless. They have nothing to gain by that action. They can be selfless due to being completely egoless. Human beings have an ego, so although many human beings can be selfless, there are varying levels of what constitutes observing selflessness. In that respect, selflessness is not of Universal Truth.

The Bright Side of Selfishness

If you believe someone else is selfish, then you're projecting a lack that exists within you. You feel everyone owes you something, which is what selfish is. You're threatened by someone who says what they want, does what they want, when they want, and without any interference. The person who is confident and goes after what they want, and who toots their own horn isn't concerned over what someone else thinks about them, especially a stranger's opinion. It will not sway the confident person who governs its life through the Light. Tooting your own horn isn't a spiritual crime. It can grow annoying for some on the receiving end when it's constant, but it's certainly not criminal. Most anyone with a social media account is praising themselves on some level. This is part of self-love, which is the opposite of low self-esteem and having no love for oneself.

An authentic selfish person has confidence and persistence. They're also less likely to be taken advantage of or give up on their goals. Selfish people have no guilt over saying no, while a narcissus will become angry when someone tells them no. Human ego trained one another to view selfishness as something negative. What some people see as selfishness, Heaven sees as self-love. Anyone calling you selfish prefers that you put yourself second and put them first, which falls into narcissism.

The opposite of being selfish is selfless, but you cannot

be adequately selfless when you've fallen into people pleasing or emotional neediness. While in that state, you become resentful that you're doing things for others and receiving nothing in return, which is not authentically selfless.

A selfish person takes care of its soul by instilling strict boundaries that prevent negative toxic people and energies from intruding on its serenity. Only when the selfish person is taken care of can they take care of others. The selfish are confident in what they want and go after it without any resistance.

The angels are selfless because they have no ego and aren't struggling to survive on a physical climate that demands you to be selfish and take care of you first. You cannot achieve great heights or survive on the planet by being entirely selfless. That's not realistic or practical in a world full of people who are untrustworthy and will take advantage of your good nature for being selfless. They'll do it in a myriad of ways from insulting you to displaying passive aggressive behavioral traits in hopes they can get you to do something for them.

A true healthy selfish person can see right through both and will have no trouble saying no without guilt. You're moving into greedy territory when you use someone for your own gain. Being selfish is not a negative trait even if it's seen that way by a narcissus. When a narcissus doesn't get what they want, or things don't go their way, they'll insist it's everyone else who is selfish only caring about themselves. You are not a victim and nobody owes you anything. You owe it to yourself to take care of you. You cannot place that kind of impossible demanding attention and love to be given to you by someone else. That's what God is for. Having confidence, integrity, strength, and going after what you want is healthy selfishness and self-love.

When you're selfish how would you know you acted selfishly? You are too self-absorbed and narcissistic to care. Learning to be selfless takes quite a bit of time. The selfish individual needs to want to become more selfless, but it's difficult for their ego to convince them that this is what should happen. There is a delicate balance between portraying both a healthy selfishness and selflessness.

How enticing it can be to attempt to keep people happy. Certain instances can call for you to people please, but if it means you're going against your higher self's integrity, or God and your Spirit team's warnings in order to do that, then your heading down precarious ground. This will create unnecessary chaos that is avoidable when you follow the wisdom you receive from above.

CHAPTER ELEVEN

The Process of Grieving from a Soul Level

Grief is part of the human experience. It can be the sadness over the death of someone close to you, but it can also be grieving over the loss of anything of value to your soul. It might be a friend or love relationship that ended. It can be losing anyone that means a great deal to you. Perhaps they moved away from you physically, mentally, emotionally, or spiritually. It can be a friend who moves away to another state or country. Even though you remain in touch, it's not the same because you're not physically hanging out in person absorbing one another's energies. The energy is more potent in person than it is through the technological waves. Grief can be present over the loss of a job or the hurt over something valuable to you. The grieving feelings one experiences with anything are the same bereaving emotion across the spectrum regardless of the circumstance. It still brings on the same pain and despair.

Being a Supportive Strength for the Grieving

Being a supportive friend to someone grieving over the physical death of a loved one can require delicate understanding. You might wrestle with whether or not you should get into spiritual talk and discuss how the soul never dies. That truth can be too far-fetched for someone to think about after they've lost someone. Deep down they may understand and already know it to be true, but it will not matter at the time they are battling with that major change in their life. Everything the one grieving usually believes is temporarily tossed out the window, because the feelings they have for the person that is no longer in front of them is so powerful. Grieving is a part of the soul's growth and experience. It must be allowed to freely feel whatever they sense in that moment without restriction or blockage.

When you're battling the depths of grief there is nothing one can truly say to you except to be there for you, to be present when needed, give space when you know the one grieving wants to be left alone. This doesn't mean vanish and disappear, but instead be within arms reach and accessible by periodically checking in. Reminding them they are not alone and that you are there.

Perhaps you're a friend who is the practical joker or the funny one who never gets that emotional. This is a gift to the grieving that needs some relief from the pain, if only for a short time. They might ask to hang out with you for the purpose of forgetting about the grief for an hour or for the day. They know you're the fun one or the jokester that is exceptional at getting everyone to forget about any stresses, sadness, or troubles. This helps in keeping their vibration high while teaching them how to laugh again.

Others grieving may want that friend who is the deep insightful one. They crave your philosophical nature. While others may want the whole gamut of friends from the funny one on Saturday, then the insightful deep one on Sunday. Some want the variety of friend experiences in order to feel the entire spectrum of emotions and understandings when it comes to the loss of someone dear.

Contrary to my work being on the more serious side, in person I'm actually more of the practical joker coupled with the philosophical insights and guidance. I've had friends going through tough grieving times in the past. When that's happened they've reached out to me that they need me to help them forget. They've spent so much time with others who are showering sympathy, but they need that no-nonsense fun time to relieve their soul of the pain.

Depending on how attached you were to the person that physically left, you will experience grief over it. The grieving emotions are still the same regardless if the person passed on in human death or physically left the relationship you had with them. It still feels like something was ripped out of you leaving you to suffocate. You feel like you cannot breath or continue on with life. You become depressed and bed ridden feeling like you want to die. Even reaching for a toxic addiction doesn't help, as you feel even more miserable afterwards. There is nothing anyone can say that can make those feelings disappear. It is the soul's individual experience to move through on their time frame.

As a supportive friend, the best you can do is be there when the grieving wants to talk, or if they want someone there in the room with them where no talking is required or necessary. They feel a comfort knowing someone else is in the house, even if you're both doing your own things in different rooms. Sometimes the grieving wants to be distracted from the feelings. They know that you can get their mind off it just by being yourself and who you typically are.

Don't beat yourself up if you're doing everything you possibly can to make them forget about it and you find it's not working. You're making them laugh, or showing them a good time, yet you look over and the person experiencing grief seems to be somewhere else and completely distracted and down. Don't take that personally, as it has nothing to do with what you're doing or not doing. You are helping them even if you're not realizing it in that moment. You're already a comfort by being there. They will appreciate that if not in the moment, but long after they've moved past the grief.

The last thing you definitely do not want to say is something along the lines of, "You need to move on." That shows you feel put out that your friend is not in the same happy content space that you are. Feeling put out is not being a genuine friend.

When you're grieving, then it becomes about you and what you've lost, and how will you go on. You will not want to go on, as it's too painful to get up everyday and put on the face that all is well, when deep down you're still in pain.

Little by little and gradually as time moves on, the wounds will heal and close, even if the scar is forever present. You will become stronger than before viewing life in a broader way through this tumultuous emotional experience. It can help you realize what's important in life. Earthly life goes beyond your job that helps pay the bills, or the material desires you continuously chase after. Suddenly everything on Earth seems trivial after you've gone through a grieving experience.

You never want to shove your personal doctrine or belief system to someone you suspect doesn't share your beliefs, or is not ready to hear it. This is regardless if it's a grieving person or not. The exception is if they ask you for that wisdom or for your take on the death.

There are many things you can do to support someone who is grieving over the death of a loved one, and that is to be a friend. Let them know you're there if they ever want to talk. Don't get into the whole soul never dies speech if they don't believe in it, or if they're not in the right state of mind to hear it. When someone is upset and feeling grief, then anything you say will not be heard much anyway.

Grieving Through a Tough Circumstance

Grieving is a state all soul's experience at one time or another when a loved one has passed away or moved on from them. It's part of the cycle of human physical life. Spirit understands that you have every good reason to be distracted when a death happens, and they will never stop communicating with you regardless. They will never stop working with you to heal your heart and help you continue on. They will work to put signs in your path that the person you lost is still around you even if you're not physically seeing them. If it's the loss of a friend, relationship, or job, then they'll work with you to help you see the loss as the beginning of something better for you.

The human experience part of you produces heavy grief at times. Sad emotions create a block with the Divine cutting off all communication. It prevents you from hearing them making it seem as if everything has gone quiet. Spirit is communicating with you especially during the grieving process, even if you're no longer picking up on anything. There is no time limit to healing as each soul has their timeline where the healing happens naturally on its own. There are positive blessings in motion outside of what seems like a tragedy and it is beauty in its simplicity.

It can be painful when someone you care about passes on, let alone when it seems they've left too soon. You worry if they've left peacefully, which is the ego creating those fears, since souls exit this plane peacefully and smoothly. It is the human existence part of you that brings in a tidal wave of grief. There is no time limit as you move through it since this process can take as long as your soul needs it to.

A Death Welcomes a New Beginning

Heart related issues are the leading cause of death in humankind. My spirit doesn't see human death in the way that others do, which is probably why I'm rarely seen typing out condolences or crying. It's not that I don't feel it because I do if it was someone close, but I don't view practical human circumstances in the same way that others might and tend to. I've been viewing it through the lens of my Spirit team, which is less emotional, but sympathetic to the pain someone is experiencing. Depending on my state of mind that day, my perception can vacillate between Spirit's eyes, then my ego's eyes, to my higher self's view, then the lower self's, and back around again. It swings all over the place like a pendulum creating a vast reservoir of emotion inside.

The morning my father passed away, the paramedics, the firemen, and the policemen that were present had all approached me in a group like a mob. One of them said, "Can we talk to you? You seem to be the only one who is together here."

That remark stood out because I hadn't given it much thought until I realized that everyone seemed to notice. It was only when they said that did I scan my surroundings realizing how upset everyone was. They added that I appeared to be standing in a calm centered focused state. I remember a Film Producer friend said once when we were working together, "You're like the calm within the storm."

You say the word "Death" to humankind and it's viewed with darkness. You do a web search of the word, "Death", and you receive pages of dark images, or the grim reaper. This is the perception humankind has of death to the point that those images are #1 on the web search engines. There is no soul death, even though the soul's experiences are met with endings and beginning's. The soul moves on and begins a new chapter, but any death is not a tragedy. It simply means your current life run is complete. Your soul continues on to a place that is much more magnificent than Earth, but mirrors that utopian ideal your soul longs for. Death shouldn't be seen as dark or negative, and I've had death throughout my life on all levels.

CHAPTER TWELVE

Healing and Transformation

The higher evolving souls on Earth move through numerous healing and transformations in one lifetime, while a baby soul may only have one long lifetime of healing and transformation that becomes clear on their Earthly death bed. Going through a healing and transformation process can be tough as you shed the old former ways of your previous life, as well as any pain accumulated that has been lodged into your soul and aura. Healing and transforming is exceptionally beneficial because it contributes to your soul's growth. You go through some rough stuff in your life, and as a result you come out of it smarter and stronger.

This doesn't mean it's necessarily fun going through all of that, but it is obligatory. If you don't experience challenges, then you don't grow. If everything is handed to you, then you risk becoming spoiled and entitled.

Healing and transforming doesn't have a timeline. It's an individual experience that can take months to years as the soul is evolving away from a certain experience. Take your time working through any healing and the emotions associated without rushing it. Avoid falling into any paths of addictions to numb the pain. All that does is put a temporary Band-Aid on it before you're eventually thrown back to the beginning in remembering the healing you were originally going through.

You'll come across feelings of loneliness and isolation. When that happens reach out to others who understand. Connect with open-minded friends that can empathize and be sympathetic. There are also support groups you can join where there are likeminded individuals going through the same thing. It doesn't feel so lonely and in fact is more familial and full of community. When going through a personal transformation you may find that you cannot relate to anybody, which is perfectly standard and normal as your soul is awakening and your consciousness is being raised in the process.

A young reader mentioned that the images I use for a social media posting tend to have only one person in them, and that it seems to symbolize loneliness. Although an interesting observation, the reasoning is because ones spiritual quest is a solo experience. When your soul is wounded, the first place it shows up is in relationships. One of the goals of the soul mates around you is to awaken something in you that needs to be addressed or caressed to life. The positive side to the more super intimate relationships you have is to help you see what needs to be dealt with within you or positively opened up. It's still an individual soul experience that is being enhanced by those around you regardless if the soul mate is a friend, acquaintance, colleague, or love relationship.

Born Into Abuse, Bullying, and Trauma

Rough life circumstances improve over time. It's tough at first, but as trite as it sounds, time does heal the painful wounds. This is the case even if you recall certain incidents that surround what caused the pain to begin with. It's not met with the same severity it had when the healing process began. You become stronger and a force to be reckoned with because of it.

Many born into abuse, bullying, or any kind of trauma tend to be stronger than others because of those experiences they endured. The dangers for some are if the damage is so great that the soul has a hard time being lifted up to do the work of going through the healing and transformation process. As a result, they could end up stuck in a permanent victim position where their life seems to be stuck on pause. You want to do the work to have an understanding of why horrible traumatic circumstances took place by moving away from blaming anyone.

Work hard to move forward fearlessly down that opened road in front of you. In the beginning, it is human nature to place blame and fault on someone else that hurt you or slighted your ego. You want to reach that place where you forgive them, so that you can let go of what happened and move forward to the next plateau. Forgiving them doesn't mean you're making excuses for their actions. On the contrary, their actions will feel unforgiveable, because it was so detestable and caused pain to others. The abuser will meet their karma at a later date and have to answer to that and pay it back in this lifetime, the other side, or the next. That will not be your problem or your issue to concern yourself with. You will forgive them for you, so that you don't have to carry around that toxicity, weight, and burden that someone else created.

You endure the varying levels of emotions one must go

through when healing and transforming. This includes understanding what brought the circumstances on to begin with. This is whether it was personal choices or a free will choice that led to the event happening.

Other considerations are if you were powerless to have been in an upsetting situation. This can be where you were a child born into a home of abuse and under the power of someone else. It wasn't a personal choice you made to be there, but you were born into it. There are two sides to every coin. One is that the soul chose to be born in a turbulent environment for a specific gain or advantage that is understood to be at a later date. This might be hard to be believed at the time. The flip side is the parent or parents operated on free will choice and from the darkness of ego. You didn't ask for it, because no one asks for horrific abuse.

I grew up in a violently abusive household where I was badly psychologically, emotionally, and physically abused by a parent. All of my relationship love partnerships ended due to the person either being uncommitted, or they strayed to the point where I ended up trusting no one. I'm on guard with anyone new I come across as I automatically expect poor behavior to be displayed. This is the cliff note version of what took place to illustrate that I understand how challenging it would or could be to reach that place where you can say, "I forgive you. I forgive you for me, because I don't want to carry this trauma and anger around for the rest of my life. I have other work to do and I wish you well on your path goodbye."

What all of those people did at the time was not okay, but I've spent years letting it go and releasing it. While there is no feeling of animosity, there are remains that I'm stuck with such as the occasional PTSD reactions that pop up out of nowhere or the social anxiety. You learn to orchestrate your life that is conducive to your well-being temperament.

As you let go of past trauma and work through it, you grow stronger and wiser. Your vibration rises, you get healthy, and you start to pay more attention to your Spirit team. You allow yourself to feel them, exercise more, hydrate, watch what you consume since that can affect one's feelings. High amounts of caffeine can heighten anxiety, while drugs or alcohol can give rise to depression feelings. Work on seeing things with a positive outlook. Circumstances happen for a reason and although that reason is not seen immediately, over time it is revealed as to why one endured a situation that called for healing and transformation.

Sometimes helping others or being of service to those in need is a positive way to get through healing. It moves your focus away from what's going on inside you and towards the donating of one's time in assisting others. It's therapeutic for one's self as well, because sometimes you're guided to help those who are in similar situations. Many great healers fall into that role because they might have had to endure some kind of past trauma or abuse. They know how to successfully navigate past that in order to help others. They have more sympathy and compassion for their patients or clients because they too had to endure that. This doesn't mean there are no healers who did not endure that either. Those ones are incarnated Earth Angel's who have the empathic psychic gifts of walking in another's shoes to get to the root of an issue.

Lead By Example

Transforming your soul includes evolving in order to see the broader picture. This helps in stripping away the ego, which causes the majority of the sabotage. When you view things from the perception of an egoless being, then you receive that clarity.

There are numerous soul lights threaded around the world doing what they can to offer reminders of the soul's path and to help other souls evolve. This may come in the form of correcting disrespectful behavior, teaching compassionate common-sense etiquette, helping someone through suffering, teaching positive spiritual concepts, helping others have a more peaceful and content life, giving and displaying love, shining at your brightest, and to allowing those in the vicinity to soak that up.

None of that is without its challenges. You're dealing with those who have an exceptionally stubborn, rigid, limited consciousness and can only see what they've been taught to date. It is rare for a human soul to branch away from how it was raised and follow their own path, since most follow what they've been taught or directed to do. There is only so much you can do to help. The best way to assist is to lead by example since you cannot force someone to bow to your whim. Not only is that against the Universal Free Will Law, but some souls will remain at the consciousness they are currently at through one Earthly lifetime.

Earthly life is a school that is freely open indefinitely for any soul looking to evolve and grow. The mediocre minds on Earth have made fun of others who seem to be buried in a book. We've seen this in Hollywood films about teens. There is always that one teenager making fun of the friend with books in her or his hand. "Why are you bringing your books?"

The one carrying those books will be going far in life we can assure you. Immersing themselves into study and research to raise and awaken their consciousness in order to transform.

Transform and Evolve

The Archangel Nathaniel tends to show up in someone's life when that person is going through a major transformation. He assists in removing anything outdated one after the other. This can include work, love, friendships, etc. It's a huge elimination, purging, and cleaning process that's taking place. This is in order to begin moving you into a new and better chapter with no additional baggage. This new chapter is more like a new book because the soul's perception of circumstances also shifts and expands as well.

Archangel Nathaniel's energy is perfect with mine as he's quite aggressive, heated and passionate in a way. He can intimidate those that might be too sensitive to that kind of energy, but I've always felt at home working with him.

Evolving souls have been choosing to incarnate since Earth's conception. At the turn of the 20th Century and beyond, the numbers of incarnations have increased astronomically to match the demand for human life choosing to procreate at an astronomical rate into the billions. This is due to poor sexual indiscretion, ignorance, peers push them to, ego rule, or because they believe God tells them it's what they're supposed to do. All are equated to having a lack of knowledge because God doesn't instruct anyone to overrun the planet to the seven billion plus and growing mark. The more human souls multiply, the more the Earthly realm souls choose to incarnate.

You may be stuck in the in-between stage of being a non-evolved soul to an evolved one, which is what the Mid-Level Souls are enduring. They are at the precipice of knowing there is much more than the mundane Earthly life than finding a job, getting married, buying a house, and having kids. An understanding is rising that there is something deeper going on with the Universe beyond what human civilization set up for physical survival.

You could be experiencing confusing and conflicting emotions about the world and wondering why you are here. You have your own personal identity and the ego part of you wants to feel important. You will do whatever it takes to obtain this. This doesn't change as you continue to transform, unless some measure of self-awareness has seeped into your consciousness.

Throughout Earth's history, humanity has continuously seen one challenging year after another unable to break free from that cycle. This is on a global level, while the individual part of you is attempting to figure out who you are and what your purpose and place is at this time. You may be searching for your own identity and wrestling with the meaning of life. Some will follow what their caregivers have instilled in them, while others will break away from that and assert their individuality to become an independent thinking human being. No matter how much you attempt to break away from what your caregivers have instilled in you, there will be traces of what your caregivers have placed upon you. It can take a lifetime to diminish the learned traits you're not proud of. You are evolving in that process. The loudest unheard voices come from the evolved. Be your own champion and walk with the Light.

Transcending Utopia

Transcending utopia is to go beyond your limits and travel outside of the generic mundane materialistic achievement that human beings taught one another to thrive for. A utopian society is what every soul secretly longs for deep down. It is where everything is perfectly blissful on all levels according to the core soul values you were born with. It isn't just outwardly perfect, but the sensations connected to how flawless everything feels reveals the authentic perfection that you were made from. Utopia is the ideal paradise as imagined in one's dreams that is also unachievable by human standards. Heaven and all of the spirit realm worlds on the Other Side is the highest form of Shangri-La, but to get close to that experience while on Earth requires a soul adjustment.

Transcending utopia is a state of mind that all spirit beings long for you to have. For some it is easy to achieve if your natural disposition state is pleasant and enjoyable, even during stressful times. It is having everything you ever dreamed of to the degree of being completely content in all ways and on all possible levels that your being has the potential for. Transcending utopia is going beyond that and even further into the distant reaches of the Universe that are impossible for the lower mind to achieve. Never give up, never lose faith, and keep forging on fearlessly towards that goal.

CHAPTER THIRTEEN

Become Your Own Messiah

As life on the planet continues to evolve and progress, so do many of the souls who choose to enter into an Earthly life. These souls are easy to spot since by the time they're about eight to twelve years old, they have begun questioning the chaos that surrounds them. They consciously know a great deal of the madness is perpetuated by the darker sides of one's self. Discovering early on that perhaps others do not have the market cornered on the point of humanity's existence. These young people are extremely sensitive and may be seen to others as different or the outcast, and hip to deception. Hence an Earth Angel is born.

Earth Angels have a larger faith based belief system beyond what organized religion has offered the previous generations. Organized religion has infused fear, doubt, guilt, and low self-esteem into others. These are qualities not aligned with God. The traits associated with Heaven are love, joy, and peace.

This isn't saying that organized religion has no light in it, as there is good in all groups and sects. The public only hears about the bad elements from each category of people. There are good people within the confines of organized religion who accept and love all with compassion as well too. Organized religions house souls who are at one level of spiritual lessons and growth.

Growing up, I loved going to the church I was a part of and had no complaints about it. There was no talk of a vengeful God and nor did anyone affiliated with the church hate or disapprove of anyone that wasn't like them. I quickly and rapidly graduated beyond that as a teenager when I realized that my connections with God were happening around the clock no matter where I was. I didn't need to go to a particular place or be around a specific group of people to connect with the other side, because my Spirit team was moving around with me wherever I went. I couldn't run from any of them, as they have always been present.

I'm aware of the hardcore religious followers that have unfortunately given Jesus Christ and Mother Mary a bad name. I don't know who they're talking about, because the way they describe Jesus and Mary is terribly inaccurate. Jesus is not some tall blonde Chris Hemsworth model with gorgeous long locks and tight abs. The real Jesus Christ that lived was short and tan.

When I went to Church regularly back in the day, I never recalled anything negative at all associated with it from the destructive words we hear today to the negative people who claim to be Jesus followers, but are in fact buried under darkness. Either I was lucky to not have heard any of that, or I was just going to the right more accepting joyful churches that are based in all love.

If I ever did hear any form of hatred, lies, or damnation, I would've left immediately. I don't tolerate that today and I most certainly didn't tolerate it then. I have no negative memories of that at the churches I went to. I also didn't grow up in that kind of a household. In fact, many family members were more agnostic and some were atheist. I was the unusual connected one, which reveals that I had come to that conclusion on my own without any family interference or influence, but rather through my Spirit connections that have been around for as long as I can remember.

There are also quite a bit of abusive organized religious sects that condemn everyone and everything in their path. They are permanently judgmental, angry, and disrespectful lacking in compassion. Bathed in lower energies, they come from a place of fear and ego, instead of God and love. They are responsible for the massively growing number of atheists threaded throughout the planet.

Many organized religious groups have been and are so abusive, negative, and hateful that they created a vast disconnection and block with God. Instead they created a closer relationship with the darkness of ego, otherwise known to them as the Devil. They were so successful in spreading false judgment out of ancient superstition that they birthed the atheist movement through this negativity. As a result, it blocked many people that grew up in that environment. You have the hate filled organized religious groups on one extreme side and then atheists on the other extreme side. Extreme sides don't bridge the gap that unites the planet together as one in compassion, unity, and love.

Someone asks their church a question about something that appears to question certain text or scripture, and no answer is given, but a generalized statement of, "Just read the Bible and follow Christ."

This is no longer an acceptable answer to the hyper intelligent souls incarnating into an Earthly life demanding answers and solutions. Because all Earth Angels operate on a higher frequency than the norm, they're suspicious and see right through organized religions that lambast and judge others that are of a different race, gender, or sexual orientation. Naïve human adults cement this into their consciousness, as if it is true Gospel.

The Bible has beautiful passages written about showing compassion and love, but then there are texts clearly written by someone residing during a superstitious time period that no longer coincides with the awakened consciousness way of thinking. Many of my guides are from the archaic days of biblical times. Some of them made significant contributions to the Bible at that time when they were living an Earthly life, such as Luke and Matthew. Much of what they discussed in those days have been modified to one degree or another, or misinterpreted.

Mother Mary, Saint of Inner Strength

Saint Mary, Mother Mary, the mother of all Mother's often depicted with the Archangel Gabriel announcing to her of the child she would deliver to humanity. They were and are both symbols of love.

In my connections with Mother Mary, I immediately discovered what a strong ferocious soul she is. This is nothing like what is depicted in man's artwork of her, which conveys softness. She is bathed in compassion, but nowhere near being like the passivity that is portrayed of her to be. Her light and presence is immense, stable, forceful, full of overflowing love, and strength like her Son's.

My relationship with Mary dates back to childhood

where I would obsessively pay homage to her image whenever I'd excitedly arrive at church as if I were going to a nightclub. A different and contradicting child, I was draped in rosary crucifixes, a filthy mouth, and a cocky arrogance that I will do what I want, when I want, without interference thank you very much.

Mary appears with this inspiring feel good inner warmth that continues to expand bigger than all the compassionate maternal beings of the world put together. The blazing sparkling rose and white light of love that shines around her outwardly like the sun is so intense that it overpowers her tiny 4'11" frame that fades into it.

The long running connection with Mary might not be surprising considering that one of my main guides Luke, who is of the Gospel of Luke, discusses Mary more than any other writer in the controversial loved and hated book. His portrait of her is layered in detail with the most quotes than any other. He's also the most educated, observant....and like myself - long winded. His stories tended to be filled with the goal of ultimate healing, which shows he had more compassion for others than some of his counterparts in the book with their superstitious fear based dogma. When touched by Mary's power, like her Son, it is unconditional love experienced that no words can describe.

Mary urges you to be strong and persevere. When you feel like crawling into a hole, you're drained, over worked, or stressed, then call on Mother Mary to help you retreat. She coaxes you not to hide and or play the victim. You will rise up and dive straight on into battle. She believes you can do it and are stronger than you may give yourself credit for. Mary has never been passive and she demands that you don't be either. When you draw from the Light, there is no telling what you cannot do. The Light helps you forge on even if you feel you're unable to. Let your connection with the Divine be the source of your pillar of strength.

Mother Nature's Wrath

When violence is placed upon the backs of anyone, then that can shake ones faith. There are good and bad people in all groups, except for terrorists who are against any and all that don't subscribe to their way of life. There is no room for light in that darkness. The real followers of God are peace loving people rather than fundamentalists or terrorists who scream the loudest and get the most attention from the media. They don't know God, but are blinded by the darkness of ego. However, deep down somewhere in that terrorists soul is someone who was born with goodness inside.

This concept has been brought to light in entertainment. Look at the *Star Wars* films, and the character Darth Vader, who was once good, but crossed over to the dark side and became evil. It wasn't until his deathbed when the goodness he once had finally came back out.

There are some who believe that Mother Nature is attempting to tell humanity something important through her majesties destruction. They find it disheartening to see so many souls passing on as a result. This includes what some consider nature's fury and anger through Earthquakes, Fires, or Hurricanes.

From a higher level, Earthquakes and other natural disasters have to do with the construction of the Earth. God or any being in Heaven doesn't make natural disasters happen, nor do they prevent them from happening. Human souls are given a place to inhabit so it's up to them to ensure it's livable. You're given a massive planet to have life on.

Like every being that exists on the planet, the planet Earth is a living-breathing organism made up of energy as every cell and atom that exists is. Energy fluctuates and compresses every second of its life reacting to the energy around it. Negative energy will aggravate all living-breathing organisms around it in a negative way since energy creates a domino effect with all that it touches.

If someone is joyful and positive, then this will uplift those around, but if they're negative and toxic, then this will bring everyone in the vicinity down. People chose to build homes on top of one another and in environments or areas that are prone to natural disasters. This isn't God's fault since He metaphorically more or less sits back and allows all souls free will to choose how they want to live life on Earth.

Nepal experienced a bad Earthquake that caused massive devastation. Many skeptics protested to ask, "Where is this alleged, God?"

My Spirit team says these areas that were destroyed were buildings that were man-made and not up to code to withstand a catastrophic Earthquake, let alone a small Earthquake. This is all due to human decision and error, not Heaven. Many people procreated at an expedited level, and then inhabited areas that cannot withstand a natural disaster. The lives lost we're not lost in spiritual truth. They passed on from this plane as a collective. When catastrophe's happen, it is the job of all Earthly souls to examine why and how it happened, rather than having the mindset that they're being punished.

The Archangel Michael can help with fear in any situation, but no one in Heaven can stop the Earth's plates from shifting. Earthquakes have been going on since the beginning of Earth's conception. Although some might claim that God controls natural disasters causing them to happen as punishment for human sin, which is ludicrous because the entire world sins. If he were controlling natural disasters for that reason, then He would take down the entire world in one clean swipe.

Planet Earth is an energy vessel and a ticking time bomb aggravated by the billions of energy atoms that encompass the souls that inhabit it. Regular disturbances such as hurricanes, fires, and earthquakes are not unusual, even though it's been extremely volatile. It cannot be denied that it's been shifting abnormally. God is not bringing in storms. It's the climate and nature that creates hurricanes. God doesn't care about possessions and homes. He cares about someone's character. When it is your time to go, it's your time.

There are also some who believe that God must love people that live in First World Countries who have access to 21st Century medicine, over those that live in Third World Countries. God doesn't control, give, or deny anything. Tragic situations happen due to human free will choice or human incompetence. Those in First World countries are not exempt from catastrophes as they've had numerous disaster's all throughout history. Some claimed that God must've hated the people of Nepal by allowing a major Earthquake to happen in 2015. The plates shifted and the Earthquake took place before anyone had a chance to pray.

It's naive to believe that God will sit there ready and able to push a button to stop a potential disaster or harm from happening simply because you want Him to. This way you can kick back, relax, and enjoy life while God sits around controlling everything to make it as pleasant and easy as possible for you. Naturally, He wants human life to be pleasant, but it's not His fault that human beings choose to govern their life through free will choice and the darkness of ego, which as a result backfires and creates harm. Who do they blame when that happens? God. He can take it regardless that it's not true.

Challenges are inevitable on Earth, and most of the time they come about due to human free will action or through a natural disaster.

Deep Thoughts On the Universe

The first man and woman that walked the planet spoke no words, but figured out what was needed to survive. They were guided to find food, shelter, and figured to clothe themselves. It isn't like the first person that roamed the planet stood up and tried on a suit. Clothes didn't exist and there was no shame with that. At one point, this changed where it was guessed, "Hmm, perhaps I should cover this area." What made him/her decide this is what should be done? If the first people that roamed the planet didn't know any better, then how would they know to do that? Where did the first man and woman come from?

While some will cite the Bible with Adam and Eve, others will cite evolution, or have various other theories. No one has the market cornered, except that there had to be a first man and woman popping up from somewhere. It wasn't like, "Poof! There they are." Did they first show up as babies? Who put them there?

Those that don't believe in a higher power are unable to answer the question in a way that would make logical sense. This planet has grown to have more than 7 billion people on it from two people, meaning we're all descendants of what some refer to be as Adam and Eve.

The first two people on the planet we're unable to read, write, or form words in speech. Language has shifted and changed over the centuries taking on an entirely different life of its own. People set up life, dictated how it should all go, and everyone else followed.

How perfectly orchestrated it is that the planets seem to glide around the sun for billions of years in a calculated succession that has been measured in technological degrees by astrologers. A human being didn't create that orchestration. A big bang theory couldn't create a perfectly orchestrated set up with planets circling the Sun for centuries never being knocked off its axis. Besides walking on the moon, no one is up in space able to accurately detect what is going on and into the further it goes.

There is this orchestrated design of the planets swirling around the Sun never being knocked off its axis where it could hurl aimlessly through space. One of those planets contains humankind, a species that has multiplied astronomically out of control into the billions. Everything is being held together by what humans call gravity, but this is a name they gave it.

How far deep into space can you go before you hit a wall? It will end at some point and circle right back around. When you come to the awareness that this universe is dangerously deep, vast, and endless, then you realize that the noise on Earth is trivial, petty, and insignificant. None of this seemingly complex design is by accident.

Astrologers have measured how the planets seem to move in particular calculated ways around the Sun. The Universe expands and goes on for eons with numerous portals that break through into the next dimension and beyond. Where did it all come from? Who set it up that way? You can't say there is no higher power and not have a valid justifiable reason as to how this Universal design exists in its exceptional perfection. Once you believe in the higher power, then you move into where the higher power came from and what it is.

Why are 7 billion people sitting on one planet alone in a

Universe with no other visible life forms anywhere else? Why do those 7 billion people share that space and spend it fighting, bickering, complaining, whining, posting, commenting, and attacking each other over ridiculousness? Human beings created that nonsense. A higher power and otherworldly figures have no time or interest for such menial trivial circumstances.

One clap in the Universe, and the Earth and everything will cease to exist. More people are growing angry in the way that others are behaving. They are welcoming something that extreme to happen to make it all go away as they've had enough. It is perplexing as to why a soul chooses to reside in the darkness of ego state around the clock. How exhausting it must be to live your life eternally in that space.

All of that and more should be the questions that every living breathing human being should be considering regardless of their personal belief systems they've chosen to follow and trust in. The answers to these questions come to life when you tune in or as you cross over back home. When that happens you realize how superficial and trivial life was on Earth. In hindsight, you kick yourself for having been sucked into it more times than you wish you had.

Only love matters, and if parents and teachers around the world all banded together to do their job of teaching love from early on, then that would bring more love like behavior to the planet. While every bit helps, every soul on this gigantic rock needs to partake in it, or the collective consciousness will be no more close to peace and love on Earth than they had ever been.

CHAPTER FOURTEEN

Philosophizing Boundless Infinite Guidance

As we wrap this up, we'll leave you with some friendly guidance reminders. This is is your life and you need to live it for you. Let no one shatter your dreams, feel no guilt about who you are, and apologize to no one about your gifts. It's no one's business how you choose to live your life. You may feel indebted to certain people in your circle this lifetime, but in higher truth the only soul you are beholden to is your own.

Live your life freely and go after what you desire with passion, enjoyment, and enthusiasm. Life may have dealt you a challenging hand, but use that to your advantage.

Challenges are not intended to punish you, but to strengthen you into a warrior. Take the hint and toughen up. Don't allow setbacks to keep you down. When you trip, stumble, and fall, then rise back up again ready to forge on into battle. Revert to faith by leaning on God and the Angels for strength and support.

Fight for your life! If there is something irking you about a decision or purchase or commitment made - then don't hesitate to taking action or feeling guilty about canceling or deleting it from your life. If a situation is leaving you to feel taken advantage of, then take steps to fix it.

Ask for Divine Assistance

There comes a point where you've done all you can do and others are using your vessel as a sponge to absorb the drama, but won't take heed of the guidance coming in. It ends up backfiring on them when you do the opposite. They come back around, "Now what do I do?"

Well, you broke the glass on the floor, so now you need to sweep up the mess. When you move through a time of a lack of clarity and a rise in anxiety, then this will cloud the messages coming in. You're not seeing the picture clearly except what your ego wants to do.

Communicate with God, Heaven, and your Angels daily. Pour your heart out to them in anyway you prefer, such as out loud, in prayer, in writing, in an email, or journal. Keep an eye out on any self-destructive tendencies you have a habit of doing, and ask for Heavenly help with it. Take it easy as much as possible is the best way to make it through.

I head out into nature regularly where all of the taxing physical energies are lifted off me. Partake in healthy activities that make you smile, whether that's cranking up some uplifting music or watching a funny movie to some lighthearted banter with a friend.

Don't give in, but keep chanting the common phrase, "This too shall pass. This too shall pass."

Because that saying is true, since everything eventually shall indeed pass away. No circumstance lasts for all eternity. When there are testy energies swirling around you, then that's a sign to take a step back and bring in God's wall of light around you to block that out. You fall into your day to day life patterns and realize, "Wait a minute. Snap me into spiritual truth."

I've certainly had those moments where I'm struggling with something for awhile, then I hear one of my spirit team members say through Clairaudience, "Do you plan on ever asking us for help on this case or are you going to continue to struggle with this on your own?"

To which I pull back, "Oh! Right. Okay."

Suddenly after asking them to help with it, it's corrected then and there by me granting permission on it.

If every single person on the planet knew or understood that there are heavenly helpers around them, then their lives would be significantly more manageable. They would view circumstances in a broader way by making sounder choices that will enhance their life even more. Having pride is by being your most authentic self and owning it.

When it comes to prayer and asking for Divine intervention and assistance, several things must be taken into account. For one, faith should be part of the equation. When doubt is included behind your words, then this can block the outcome. Remember to include genuine gratitude for the blessings you currently have. When your prayers are all about what Heaven can give you, then how do you think that looks? What are you contributing to help matters along?

Another factor is to pay attention to what you're psychically or intuitively picking up on from God and Spirit. What action steps are you being asked to do? Sometimes you may be asked to step outside of your comfort zone. This can create fear and anxiety prompting you to procrastinate and push off doing it, because you're too full of anxiety surrounding that action step. Have no fear and charge on in with what you want. This is your life and you are the owner of it.

If it's another job you want, you may be asked to make a call, or send an email to someone that can help. When you play the Earthly game, then you're more apt to receiving your wishes and blessings. Ask for an increase of faith from above when you feel it waning.

Call in the Archangel Michael to extract all fear and anxiety from your aura if you're called to transform into a warrior and grab what you want without hesitation. Don't allow other people to hold you back from your dreams and desires.

Fear Not, Because I Am With You

Who is this being of Light so great it has conjured up centuries of endless controversy and hatred in the darkness of human ego. The irony is that He is nothing that comes close to that limited view. His light has the opposite effect when you are truly standing in His presence.

Despite the toxic noise that pervades Earth by human kind, this most holy child of salvation's eminence never stops illuminating love and healing energy light off his radiance. His power and Light are so magnificent and so intense that I've had to stop whatever I was doing when he's entered my vicinity because his presence is so overwhelming that it's paralyzing. Words to describe what's taking place never do it justice. It's a sense feeling of the highest most impossible love that I've never seen another human being give, but he did and he does.

If you're down and out or experiencing any negative thought or feeling, His love can wipe that away just by walking into your room and standing next to you. Find that space where his love resides and bathe in its vitality. The planet could learn a little something about this unconditional healing love He continuously gives without censure in a world devoid of respect.

Out of the deepest dark shines the purest light that blasts away all traces of negativity, anger, sadness, confusion, and stress from your being. If there's anything good that happens in life, it's from God. He is present for all who call on him regardless of who you are, what you believe in, or your souls choices this lifetime. All are welcome to His love without judgment. You have His uncompromising permanent compassion and friendship. You are loved in ways your ego is incapable of understanding or comprehending. Those without love, those who are troubled, those wrestling with demons, you are forever loved by this being of Light free of charge. Hookers and drug users have someone who loves them unconditionally, because no one on the planet is exempt from His love.

It's less shocking to the soul that has crossed over to first see a figure they identified with on Earth. To go from a human life on Earth, to human death, is surprising for some. The deity they believed in or followed on Earth will appear first after death to ease them into the other plane. If you followed all deities on an equal measure, then all of them would surface. Heaven knows your consciousness and the one you would gravitate towards when it is your time to cross through the gates back home.

Why am I here? You might ask. There's very little

that's pleasant about this place. One of the messages Jesus said was that even just a tiny bit of faith that you can spare will move mountains.

"Nothing would be impossible."

His love for you is boundless regardless if you're a believer or not. He doesn't need faith to believe in you. He already does. It already is.

What did God say? "Fear not, because I am with you."

There's nothing you can't do when you've got your Spirit team in your house.

Affirm always: I am worthy. I deserve good. I deserve blessings. I deserve love. I deserve to be happy. I deserve peace.

Understanding Love

Some souls incarnate into an Earthly life wanting to experience all of Earthly physical pleasures from sex, food, and music, making love, falling in love, loving love. Love is an in-depth complicated word to describe. One hears the word 'love' and automatically assumes it's, "I love you." What love is in general is difficult to pin down since the meaning is much deeper than the surface. It's an intense satisfying appreciation for someone or something, or an approving supportive expression for someone or something. Love is more than love and relationships. It's putting love into whatever you do. It's making choices from the heart, rather than rationalizing it through the mind, which can talk you out of doing something you are more than capable of.

Love is to understand that even the most heinous person in your eyes has love built into them deep down. There is no such thing as Universal love. You may find someone to be monstrous, while another person has a deeper understanding of that person. Someone tells me about someone that enacted a horrible crime. While others immediately jump into the hang him rhetoric, I calmly grow fascinated with the complexities of a human being and all of the details that it encompasses.

Channel Anger Positively

Take any anger and channel it positively through action. This action should be intended to fix whatever it is you're angry about, otherwise let it go. Being angry at someone else isn't going to make them change. They're off busy happily doing their thing while you're at home bitter and irritated marinating in that toxic cesspool energy that only hurts your well-being.

Stand up and speak out in ways that can benefit others positively. This isn't to be confused with vocally complaining or gossiping about something, which is lower vibrational negative energy that does nothing to benefit anyone at all ever. If something is bothersome and you feel the need to vent or complain, then turn the words into action statements that can improve matters.

If you're truly interested in rising above an issue, then you will communicate in ways that will resolve it so that you can continue moving forward fearlessly instead of remaining stuck in the quick sand of toxicity. Honor your higher self's truth and wishes, which includes speaking your truth with assertiveness and compassion.

Be fearless and stand up for yourself and ask for what you want, whether it is from your Spirit team or those in life that can help you. This can be for something like getting another job to finding the right love partner.

Dissolve all of the layers of negativity you've accumulated so that you can bring that part of your life to closure. Start a bright new chapter with a clean slate, fresh, and vibrantly informed. Create more suitable solutions for yourself that will make you infinitely happier in the end. Never do or say anything just to make someone feel better if it makes you feel less than your stellar self by doing so.

Get Unstuck From the Rut

Many around the world continue to feel stuck. They are in the middle of a transition or they're at a crossroads evaluating all aspects of their lives that cause unhappiness. They know changes need to take place in their lives. There is going to be quite a bit of moving on as far as changes go for them. Leaving one way of life and into another. This includes a great deal of people walking away from their current employment and into another one, or leaving one relationship and into another. Many will be making moves to improve their lives. This includes adopting a more balanced point of view.

It is time to work on getting unstuck and work on changing your perception of world events as well as personal ones. Incorporate positive healthy life changes and viewpoints. Tune into the higher vibrations of spirit to see the truth of why events and circumstances take place. Negative anything harms your health, whether that be your feelings or thoughts, so always revert to shedding the negative layers you continue to add around you.

Cause and Effect

Model yourself as the creator and as the angels do. They love you without conditions, which means there is nothing any being can say or do to stop that love no matter how horrific. This doesn't mean negative actions are without consequence since each being is creating their own reality everyday. They are paying for both positive and poor actions previously made.

What is put out into the Universe is flipped around and multiplied right back to you in this lifetime, the next, and the other worlds and planes beyond. It's the nature of the way that the Universe is laid out. The energy will catch up with you whether you choose to follow the herd as a collective and partake in negative actions, or out of your own independence. The ego drops down into darkness when it has a group to feed off of. It is more likely to contribute negatively to the violent energy being emitted outwardly into the Universe when joining a group to hide behind over hitting the pavement solo.

Every action made has an effect, so in essence the actions you make today are bending the energy around you forming new circumstances that are of equal or greater value to that energy. Regardless if the energy you send out into the ethers is positive or negative, it will multiply. Sometimes what is manifested from that energy can happen almost immediately, while other times it can take anywhere from three to six months on average to transpire.

Accept the Things You Cannot Change

Use an equal balance of logic and emotion. This isn't to be confused with being closed off emotionally with others. This is about avoiding the long fall into the abysmal whirlwind of wasted emotions over something trivial such as a news story, unless you're able to practically do something positive about it. The complaints and constant attacking of others that so many partake in today do nothing to help anyone, except contribute to the noise.

There will continue to be a greater divide, opposing viewpoints, arguments, conflict, and challenges brought on by the darkness of ego. Earthly life will continue to be more of a repeat for those stuck in that rigid mindset. None of that will help to bridge opposing viewpoints until those who are guilty of it learn about the true meaning of having compassion and displaying respect for others. This also means showing those virtues to those you disagree with. It's looking for ways to meet an opponent in the middle.

Avoid obsessing over a media headline as that lowers your vibration, which creates a block. There is nothing positive gained by becoming emotionally invested in a news story. That is the overall theme of modern day life today in the post technological age, which is discussed in my book, *Monsters and Angels*. It's time to move the held back consciousness away from that.

There are those who spend each year wishing the previous year would go away. Reality is what you make it, so if you choose to see a year as being miserable, then that's the energy you'll continue to bring in. Moving forward is not going to change anything until you decide to change.

What is one of the steps in Alcoholics Anonymous? God, grant me the serenity to accept the things I cannot change. The courage to change the things I can and the wisdom to know the difference.

Have the perception of a great actor, which is to walk in another's shoes as if you are part of their consciousness. All of this can help in raising your vibration, which will give you stronger psychic input.

Move Towards the Direction of Your Dreams

Acquire knowledge and wisdom through the process of living and feeling good about how it all ends up. Make the decision to change your ships course and instead aim your soul towards the direction of your dreams. The things you say and do now set in motion what is to come six months to a year from that point, so be aware and conscious of what it is you are putting out into the Universe.

Take the occasional step back to take stock in how your life has gone to date. Notice all of what you've accomplished. Examine your triumphs, your sorrows, your successes, and your challenges. What was lost and what was gained? Look forward to the next six months of your life and affirm that it will go with superior promise. You will do your best to ensure that it will be even better than it's ever been.

Looking to the future with optimism you might sometimes find you've been chasing mirages that evaporate as quickly as the champagne fizzles in your glass. You need not search long and hard for some measure of magic to reveal itself since it's always resided within you.

Focus on the Good In Your Life

Every morning you wake up, have gratitude for what you have now, then mentally say to your consciousness that you will make today count.

One exercise can be to find an empty jar or canister, get a stack of post-its or little notes, and leave those blank notes next to the jar. At least once a week write at least one awesome thing that happened for you that week or each day. Even if it was someone who showered you with a smile that stuck. Fold up the little note and put it in the jar. Every so often, we'll say six months, pull all of the little notes out and read each one and notice the blessings and good things that actually did take place in your life that you might have normally brushed off. Some people focus only on lack or what went wrong, but one rarely shines light on all of the good that took place.

Focus on the good things that happen in your life that might seem miniscule because it's not the big lottery financial win. If you get a flat tire that ruined your day, don't talk about that aspect of it on the post-it, but instead mention who intervened to help your day brighten up, even if it was the tow truck driver that got you up and running again. There are blessings all around you when you take the time to notice them.

Re-centering Yourself

The voices of spirit are uplifting and calm, even if it is warning you of danger. They will guide, inspire, and lovingly coax you onward on your higher self's path. Their intention is to help you stay focused and clear minded in order to accomplish your life purpose goals. They're not fans of seeing anyone experience negative emotions and therefore desire to help you swiftly move past that when it hits you. It's part of the human condition to have easy access to these feelings, since that is the doorway to communicating with Spirit. When the negative emotions over take you, then this blocks communication and does more harm than good to your overall well-being.

Even the most centered person on the planet experiences negative feelings from time to time. When that happens, they can readily glide over it and move back into a focused detached emotional state, rather than dwelling in the toxicity of negative emotions. Address something with assertive compassion that needs to be addressed, then let it go and move on.

The centered soul is in tune and can easily hone in on the reasoning behind someone's actions that might have bothered them to begin with. They do this without judgment. This isn't about making excuses for someone's poor behavior, but it's understanding what's behind an action and choosing not to be a part of any blame, drama, or anything that brings you down or negatively riles you up. When you move into negative territory, then revert to focusing on activities and people that make you smile. The clearer Divinely guided answers come in when you're standing still.

Meditate, relax, and center yourself guru. Drink more water than usual to release the toxins accumulated in your organs, but in your emotional state as well. Things begin to feel good after you release the junk that clogs up your soul. It's healing, therapeutic, and freeing. When the Divinely guided answers come in, then follow it.

Lighten Up, Have Fun, and Love More

Derive pleasure out of the things you love the most. Don't allow any stress or negativity to override this pleasure. This also means avoid engaging in anything that's going to bring you misery. Focus on the good and the uplifting. Go after what you want without reservation. The happier you allow yourself to become, then the healthier you are. This equates to a longer more fulfilling, passionate, joyous life. This is what every soul wants and deserves.

Incorporate regular bouts of fun times, make and connect with friends, family, and acquaintances. Open up and be sociable with others without any demands.

Connecting with others through lightheartedness gives you a joy boost, which then raises your vibration. A high vibration is what brings positive manifestations into your life. Being sociable has added health benefits including that of being a wonderful stress reliever. This version of sociability with others does not mean resorting to gossip, slander, and complaints, but rather choosing to enjoyably engage with other people's energies. Seek out camaraderie, community, and positive shifts. Open up your heart to others with love and affection.

You are loved even when you doubt it, avoid it, shun it and do everything in your power to deny it. When you reach that threshold of completing your run, the only thing you take with you is love. If you gain any knowledge of value, remember to love more, give more, and have compassion no matter how unpopular it's become. Only then can you truly discover that magic your soul secretly desires.

Rejoice and Celebrate Your Life

If God raised you, then you would grow up to see the love in all souls. You would exude love and joy full time. The best parts of you are what God is, and the worst parts are the darkness of your ego.

Practice with starting each day on a high note, since that will set the tone for the next twenty-four hours. How often have you woken up in a negative mood only to find that's carried into the rest of the day? Your coffee machine won't work, you're running late for work, and discover the traffic is worse than it's ever been. You walk into work and thrown at you are one issue after another. By the time you get out of work agitated, you race home to have a drink.

Rejoice, celebrate, and love all that you are inside and out. You are perfect and beautiful through the eyes of God and the angels. This love for your soul is unconditional. See yourself in this same light as Heaven sees you and remember to practice self care. You are intended for greatness. If you never do anything else, but let your loving light shine through to the world, then that will be enough to help combat all the evil in the world.

Your life moves in cycles that fluctuate. You can detect when an official cycle is ending due to all of the back to back closing of doors that appears to be happening. This can cause you to be filled with enormous tension. Allow the doors that need to be closed to do so as it is prepping you for a new chapter. You can use that time spent retreating, laying low, gathering knowledge, purging, and centering, so that you may rise in strength with clarity for your next new chapter.

Personal changes are much like the cycles of the weather seasons that ebb and flow. You are moving through a series of chapters, peaks, and valleys every day. Those are great times to evaluate and probe deeper into what you've experienced to date, how you've grown, what you've learned, and how you'll choose to move forward. What will you leave behind and what will you take with you on the next part of your soul's journey onward and upward into Utopia and beyond?

Reach a Higher Awareness Level

There is goodness threaded out amidst the darkness of the world, and the good deeds taking place out there are enacted without the desire for anything in return. Because it's seemingly rare, when it does happen you're floored and prompted to take a step back in stunned amazement,

"Wow!"

The love available from above never ceases all throughout any personal ordeal. This is also to help face the soul in the direction of this source of love. It's only hoped the soul can snap back into the true higher consciousness to realize that none of the drama around them matters. Nor is it based in reality because you've given your power away to a ruler or a group thinking they have jurisdiction to help you feel better.

Those good feelings you're attempting to access are already built into you and are available for accessibility. You don't need the group to prop you up in the end. Maybe you did in the beginning as you wear the training armor to get your feet wet and become strong, but in the end it was never needed. One of the premises in the Disney film, "Dumbo", was he never needed the magical feather to fly. He was always able to fly without it.

You might show love to the Universe, your guides, your team, God, and all in Heaven, but it's not because they are soaking up the love you return tenfold. They have no ego and have no desire for those elements because that love is already built into them. The love essence is their true nature, so they don't desire something they already have. Those same love elements are also a part of every soul on Earth, even though it might seem as if someone has strayed far away from it through poor actions, behavior, or cruel words. Heaven is so busy loving that they are impartial to whether or not you love them back.

Reaching that moment of awareness and awakening is one of the greatest gifts you can give your soul. You become that much closer to transcending utopia. A personal awakening is like the rapture where the trumpet blows, and the sky parts, and the Archangel descends with a shout! This is the moment when light is shed onto your consciousness and you see things you hadn't noticed before. The answer was always there, but it was as if you were previously living in darkness. It's a beautiful incredible feeling reaching that state of knowingness. The truth was always in front of you, but you hadn't paid much attention to it until that moment of awareness that feels like a magnificent exhilarated release. Only then are you taking your first baby steps into utopia

ALSO BY KEVIN HUNTER

Warrior of Light
Empowering Spirit Wisdom
Darkness of Ego
Realm of the Wise One
Transcending Utopia
Reaching for the Warrior Within
Spirit Guides and Angels
Soul Mates and Twin Flames
Raising Your Vibration
Divine Messages for Humanity
Connecting with the Archangels
The Seven Deadly Sins
A Beginner's Guide to the Four Psychic Clair Senses
Tarot Card Meanings
Living For the Weekend
Monsters and Angels
Love Party of One
Ignite Your Inner Life Force
Awaken Your Creative Spirit
The Essential Kevin Hunter Collection

The Essential Kevin Hunter Collection
Available in Paperback and E-book

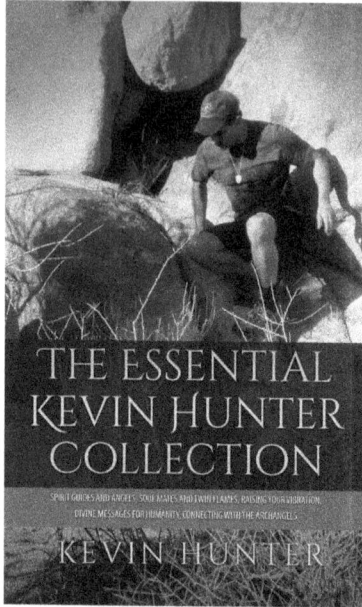

THE ESSENTIAL
KEVIN HUNTER
COLLECTION

Featuring the following books:
Warrior of Light, Empowering Spirit Wisdom, Darkness of Ego,
Spirit Guides and Angels, Soul Mates and Twin Flames, Raising
Your Vibration, Divine Messages for Humanity, and Connecting
with the Archangels.

Living for the Weekend
*The Winding Road Towards Balancing
Career Work and Spiritual Life*
Available in Paperback and E-book

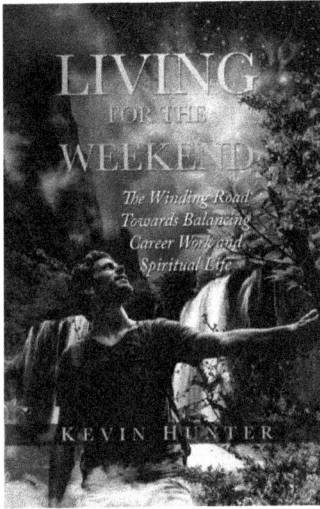

Working hard to ensure your bills are paid can leave your soul spiritually starved for soul nourishment. When your ultimate goal is to obtain enough money to be comfortable that you become carried away in that current, then there is little to no room for Divine enrichment.

Many work to survive in jobs they hate because it's the way it is. As a result, they experience and endure all sorts of emotional pain whether it is through depression, sadness, anger, or any other kind of negative stressor. Some silently suffer through this emotional strain gradually killing off their life force. If you don't have a healthy social life and positive fun filled activities and hobbies to balance that burden outside of that, then that can add additional tension. What's it all for if you can't live the life you've always wanted to live? Instead, you spend your days growing forever miserable and broken.

Living for the Weekend examines the pitfalls, struggles, as well as the benefits available in the current modern day working world. This is followed up with spiritual and practical tips, guidance, messages, and discussions on ways to incorporate more balance and enlightenment to a cutthroat material driven world.

WARRIOR OF LIGHT
Messages from my Guides and Angels

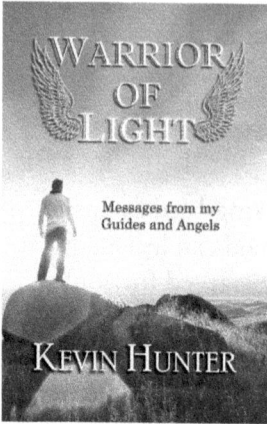

There are legions of angels, spirit guides, and departed loved ones in heaven that watch and guide you on your journey here on Earth. They are around to make your life easier and less stressful. Do you pay attention to the nudges, guidance, and messages given to you? There are many who live lives full of negativity and stress while trying to make ends meet. This can shake your faith as it leads you down paths of addictions, unhealthy life choices, and negative relationship connections. Learn how you can recognize the guidance of your own Spirit team of guides and angels around you. Author, Kevin Hunter, relays heavenly guided messages about getting humanity, the world, and yourself into shape. He delivers the guidance passed onto him by his own Spirit team on how to fine tune your body, soul and raise your vibration. Doing this can help you gain hope and faith in your own life in order to start attracting in more abundance.

EMPOWERING SPIRIT WISDOM
*A Warrior of Light's Guide on Love,
Career and the Spirit World*

Kevin Hunter relays heavenly, guided messages for everyday life concerns with his book, *Empowering Spirit Wisdom*. Some of the topics covered are your soul, spirit and the power of the light, laws of attraction, finding meaningful work, transforming your professional and personal life, navigating through the various stages of dating and love relationships, as well as other practical affirmations and messages from the Archangels. Kevin Hunter passes on the sensible wisdom given to him by his own Spirit team in this inspirational book.

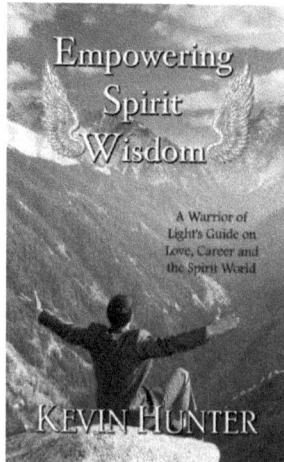

DARKNESS OF EGO

In *Darkness of Ego*, author Kevin Hunter infuses some of the guidance, messages, and wisdom he's received from his Spirit team surrounding all things ego related. The ego is one of the most damaging culprits in human life. Therefore, it is essential to understand the nature of the beast in order to navigate gracefully out of it when it spins out of control. Some of the topics covered in *Darkness of Ego* are humanity's destruction, mass hysteria, karmic debt, and the power of the mind, heaven's gate, the ego's war on love and relationships, and much more.

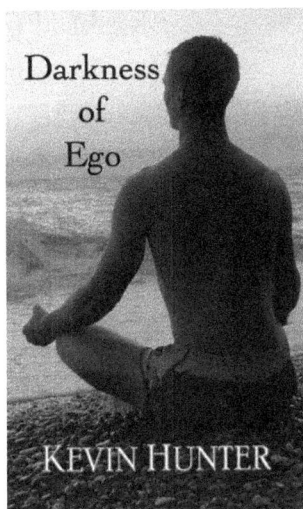

REACHING FOR THE WARRIOR WITHIN

Reaching for the Warrior Within is the author's personal story recounting a volatile childhood. This led him to a path of addictions, anxiety and overindulgence in alcohol, drugs, cigarettes and destructive relationships. As a survival mechanism, he split into many different "selves". He credits turning his life around, not by therapy, but by simultaneously paying attention to the messages he has been receiving from his Spirit team in Heaven since birth.

REALM OF THE WISE ONE

In the Spirit Worlds and the dimensions that exist, reside numerous kingdoms that house a plethora of Spirits that inhabit various forms. One of these tribes is called the Wise Ones, a darker breed in the spirit realm who often chooses to incarnate into a human body one lifetime after another for important purposes.

The *Realm of the Wise One* takes you on a magical journey to the spirit world where the Wise Ones dwell. This is followed with in-depth and detailed information on how to recognize a human soul who has incarnated from the Wise One Realm. Author, Kevin Hunter, is a Wise One who uses the knowledge passed onto him by his Spirit team of Guides and Angels to relay the wisdom surrounding all things Wise One. He discusses the traits, purposes, gifts, roles, and personalities among other things that make up someone who is a Wise One. Wise Ones have come in the guises of teachers, shaman, leaders, hunters, mediums, entertainers and others. *Realm of the Wise One* is an informational guide devoted to the tribe of the Wise Ones, both in human form and on the other side.

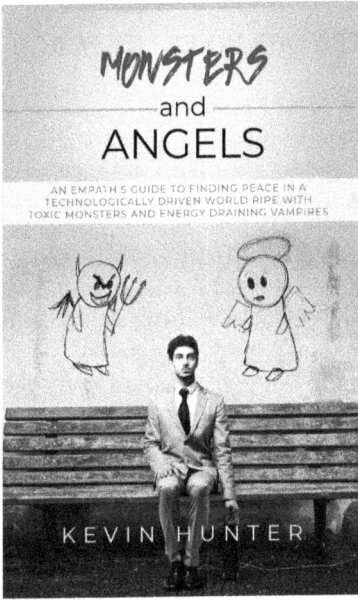

MONSTERS AND ANGELS

An Empath's Guide to Finding Peace in a Technologically Driven World Ripe with Toxic Monsters and Energy Draining Vampires

Every person on the planet is capable of being empathic and sensitive, to becoming an energy vampire or toxic monster. No one is exempt from displaying the darker sides of their ego. The easiest and most efficient way to spread any kind of energy is online. Every time you log onto the Internet, there is a larger chance you're going to see something related to the news, media, or gossip areas thrown in front of you, even if you attempt to avoid it as much as possible. You're absorbing everything that your consciousness faces, including the ugly and the wicked, which has its own consequences. This tempestuous energy is tossed into the Universe ultimately creating a flame-throwing battleground inside and around you.

Monsters and Angels discusses how technology, media, and social media have an immense power in distributing both positive and negative influences far and wide. This is about being mindful of what can negatively affect your state of being, and how to counter and avoid that when and wherever possible. This is why it's beneficial to govern yourself, your life, and your surroundings like a strict disciplined executive.

Some of the topics discussed include: *Energy vampires, toxic monsters, sensitive angels, and empaths, the technological craze, being sensitive in a technical driven world, connecting through technical means, the insanity of the ego, steering clear of drama, finding balance in the media, technological detox tips, rising above the mundane and into the Divine, climbing beyond superficiality, and centering your inner light.*

IGNITE YOUR INNER LIFE FORCE

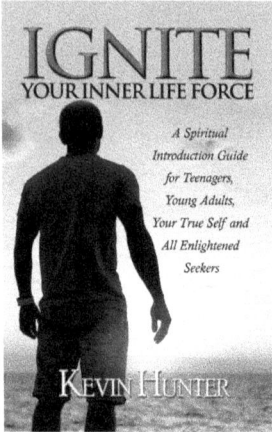

Ignite Your Inner Life Force is an introduction guide for teens, young adults, and anyone seeking answers, messages, and guidance and surrounding spiritual empowerment. This is from understanding what Heaven, the soul, and spiritual beings are to knowing when you are connecting with your Spirit team of Guides and Angels. Some of the topics covered are communicating with Heaven, working with your Spirit team, what your higher self is, your life purpose and soul contract, what the ego is, love and relationships, your vibration energy, shifting your consciousness and thinking for yourself even when you stand alone. This is an in-depth primer manual offering you foundation as you find a higher purpose navigating through your personal journey in today's modern day practical world.

AWAKEN YOUR CREATIVE SPIRIT

Your creative spirit is more than being artistic and getting involved in creativity pursuits, although this is a good part of it. When your creative spirit is activated by a high vibration state of being, then this is the space you create from. You can apply this to your dealings in life, your creative and artistic pursuits, and to having a greater communication line with your Spirit team on the Other Side. *Awaken Your Creative Spirit* is an overview of what it means to have access to Divine assistance and how that plays a part in arousing the muse within you in order to bring your state of mind into a happier space.

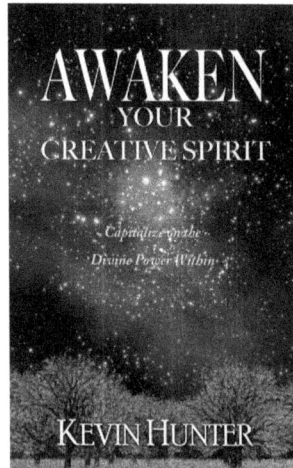

The *Warrior of Light* series of pocket books are available in paperback and E-book called, *Spirit Guides and Angels, Soul Mates and Twin Flames, Divine Messages for Humanity, Raising Your Vibration, Connecting with the Archangels,* and *The Seven Deadly Sins*

TAROT CARD MEANINGS

A Beginner's Guide to the
FOUR PSYCHIC CLAIR SENSES

Learn about the four main psychic clair senses to help you connect with Heaven, the Spirit World, and the Other Side. Take that one step further and use those senses to read the Tarot! *Tarot Card Meanings* is an encyclopedia reference guide that takes the Tarot apprentice reader through each of the 78 Tarot Cards offering the potential general meanings and interpretations that could be applied when conducting a reading, whether it be spiritual, love, general, or work related questions. This is an easy to understand manual for the Tarot novice that is having trouble interpreting cards for themselves, or a Tarot reader who loves the craft and is looking for a refresher or another point of view. The *Four Psychic Clair Senses* focuses on the main channels that Heaven and Spirit communicate with you. *Both books are available in Paperback and E-book wherever books are sold.*

About Kevin Hunter

Kevin Hunter is an author, love expert, and channeler. His books tackle a variety of genres and tend to have a strong male protagonist. The messages and themes he weaves in his work surround Spirit's own communications of love and respect, which he channels and infuses into his writing work.

His spiritually based empowerment books include *Warrior of Light, Empowering Spirit Wisdom, Realm of the Wise One, Reaching for the Warrior Within, Darkness of Ego, Transcending Utopia, Living for the Weekend, Ignite Your Inner Life Force, Awaken Your Creative Spirit,* and *Tarot Card Meanings*. His metaphysical pocket books series include, *Spirit Guides and Angels, Soul Mates and Twin Flames, Raising Your Vibration, Divine Messages for Humanity, Connecting with the Archangels, The Seven Deadly Sins, Four Psychic Clair Senses* and *Monsters and Angels*. He is also the author of the dating singles guide *Love Party of One*, the horror/drama, *Paint the Silence,* and the modern day erotic love story, *Jagger's Revolution.*

Before becoming an author, Kevin started out in the entertainment business in 1996 as the personal development guy to one of Hollywood's most respected talent, Michelle Pfeiffer, for her boutique production company, Via Rosa Productions. She dissolved her company after several years and he made a move into coordinating film productions for the studios on such films as *One Fine Day, A Thousand Acres, The Deep End of the Ocean, Crazy in Alabama, The Perfect Storm, Original Sin, Harry Potter & the Sorcerer's Stone, Dr. Dolittle 2,* and *Carolina.* He considers himself a beach bum born and raised in Southern California. For more information, www.kevin-hunter.com